WAKEFIELD PRESS

Can a Duck Swim?

To Marrie Lou.
With Best Wishes &
fond Memories.

June.

Can a Duck Swim?

An Autobiography

JUNE PORTER

Wakefield Press

Wakefield Press
1 The Parade West
Kent Town
South Australia 5067
www.wakefieldpress.com.au

First published 2013

Designed by Liz Nicholson, designBITE
Edited by Laura Andary, Wakefield Press
Typeset by Wakefield Press
Printed and bound in China by Broad Link Enterprise Ltd

National Library of Australia Cataloguing-in-Publication entry

Author: Porter, June.
Title: Can a duck swim?: an autobiography / June Porter.
ISBN: 978 1 74305 201 3 (hbk.).
Subjects: Porter, June.
Women – Western Australia – Perth – Biography.
Diplomatic and consular service, Australian – India – History.
India – Social life and customs – 1919–1947.
Dewey Number: 994.04092

FOR TOM

CONTENTS

Foreword

So much of history is the story of the powerful; of kings and queens, of presidents and prime ministers. Even published autobiographies are dominated by the powerful. Yet history is made up of much more than leaders. There are the daily participants in social life, the observers of society's steady evolution and facilitators of human interaction.

Every so often someone comes along with a book based on these experiences that, with clarity and precision, opens the door to a world that has passed. *Can a Duck Swim* is one of those books. It is the fascinating story of a woman who has lived through the Depression, war and the passing of Empire, not as a principal actor but as a privileged observer.

June Porter, née Perry, grew up in the comfortable world of the Perth bourgeoisie during the 1920s and 1930s. She paints a picture of a loving family and a lively Perth social scene in those days before the horrors of war gripped Australia and the world. She helps us understand how many people lived through those years without the ease of the transport and communications that we enjoy today. June met a young Adelaide man, Tom Porter; they fell in love but were separated by the Nullarbor Plain. Getting from Perth to Adelaide and keeping in touch when separated were no easy tasks.

Then it was war, though that brought with it not just drama and sorrow but also opportunity. Tom went to India as an ADC to the only Australian who governed part of British India, Richard Casey. In later years, Casey went on to serve as Australian foreign minister for nine years before becoming the Governor-General of Australia.

The most fascinating part of this book is the wonderful insight it gives the modern reader into pre-independence India. First and foremost are the palaces. The British governors lived like princes in huge buildings with servants to attend to their every need. June enjoyed with wry amusement the rich social life of these rulers of the world's second most populous country. At first she was taken aback by its protocol and pomposity – so unlike Australia. But despite that, she and Tom were able to hold their own even with the likes of Lord and Lady Mountbatten.

And the reader will enjoy the tales of tiger shooting in an era when the notion of endangered species was largely unknown.

We are reminded of how the British ruled India. This was a British India directly ruled by Britons with the support of a proficient Indian civil service and army. We forget that only the most senior civil servants and soldiers were British. The rest were Indians.

We are also reminded that part of India was ruled by Maharajas, super-rich princes whose palaces and Bentleys and Rolls Royces put even the British governors to shame. But woven through the narrative about India is the sense that it was all coming to an end; there were riots and broader agitation, which led to Britain's withdrawal from India in 1947.

June and Tom had left the country before then and made a fascinating visit to both France and Britain soon after the end of the war. These were societies devastated and determined to rebuild themselves. And they wanted to do so with a sense of enjoyment; society continued to operate albeit in straitened circumstances.

And then the Porters returned to Adelaide. They became the heart and soul of the city's social life, eventually rising to the lofty positions of Lord Mayor and Lady Mayoress.

June Porter was Adelaide's *grande dame*. And she still is. It's a great thing that she has written her memoirs of a very long and fascinating life. This book helps us all understand the tumultuous events of the twentieth century through the eyes of an intelligent and insightful woman. It's a fascinating story.

The Honourable Alexander Downer
September 2012

Preface

Having regaled friends and almost anyone who would listen with stories of my life and especially of my time living in India during the last days of the British Raj, all enthusiastically urged me to write about my experiences, no doubt with the object of keeping me quiet! I always said that I was saving that for my wheelchair. But as it is only pure bloody mindedness that is keeping me from a wheelchair, I have decided to take up the challenge anyway.

This is really the story of a young girl who went from the suburbs of Perth to live in palaces in India with people who were making history. How and why this came about necessitates relating something of my former life and the period after to provide a broader context. This story is taken from the letters I wrote regularly to my family, and which my mother kept, my diaries and those of my husband, Tom, and a host of photographs. It must be remembered that the times about which I am writing depict an entirely different way of life and thinking; they describe a world that has now gone and must be taken in that context.

It has been an extremely emotional journey reliving my life of sixty-eight years ago; I have been in a time capsule these last months, with the life that I have lived being still so vivid in my mind. And if asked would I have my life all over again, I would certainly say, 'Can a duck swim?'

June Porter
October 2012

CHAPTER 1

Life before India

On Friday 8 September 1944 at 8 am, I stood on the deck of the SS *Glenartney* as it drew slowly from the wharf at Fremantle, Western Australia. No throngs of friends were cheerfully calling 'Bon voyage' or throwing rolls of coloured streamers from shore to ship to make a fluttering sea of colour on which to look down and cheer me on my way. Only my parents were there – two lone figures standing on the wharf below. Australia was at war and all maritime movements were shrouded in secrecy. The Colombo-bound unescorted *Glenartney* was a merchant ship carrying war supplies, army and navy personnel, four American women rejoining husbands who worked with Standard Oil Company in India, and me, and we were about to set sail into the Indian Ocean.

The Indian Ocean had a grizzly record when it came to the number of ships sunk during the period 1942–1944, with six Allied and British ships sunk in the month I sailed. One of those sunk was the SS *Behar* in March 1944. Most of the crew and passengers were murdered on board, and Rear Admiral Naomase Sakongi was executed after the war for this crime. So not surprisingly my mother was distraught and felt sure I was going to a watery grave. But I was young and buoyed by the significance of the period in history in which I was living.

After the farewells, I went down to breakfast, and returned to the deck with mixed emotions. As I watched the golden coastline of Australia gradually recede into the distance, one part of me wanted to jump over and return to the safety and warmth of home and family, while the other was filled with elation that at last I was on my way to rejoin my husband, Tom. As I sailed away into the Indian Ocean, I reflected on my life so far, with all its coincidences which had brought me, like Alice in Wonderland, a girl from the suburbs of Perth, on her way to a mystical, exotic country to live in palaces with people who were making history, and to a life about which one only read or dreamt.

Early days

I was born on 20 March 1919 in Melbourne to Hilda and Stan Perry, who were wonderful parents and provided much loving care and every possible opportunity in life. On 7 July 1924, my little sister Shirley joined us, and I believe my nose was severely put out of joint. Having been the sole focus of my parents' lives for nearly six years the attention now moved to the new baby. However, there was soon to be another diversion as my father was offered, and accepted, an appointment with the Hoyts cinema chain in Sydney (his father, Joseph Henry Perry, had been a pioneer of the Australian film industry).

In Sydney I started school at Kambala, a Church of England girls' school at Rose Bay. Kambala was a large, grey stone building on the curve of Old South Head Road that wound towards Watsons Bay, with large playing fields and sweeping harbour views. My life was filled with new friends, school activities and sport – I seem to have no recollection of schoolwork at all! On these beautiful playing fields I had my first tennis lessons and my love of sport flourished.

From an early age I thought I knew everything, including that there was no Father Christmas and every Christmas Eve Daddy consumed all the beer and cake we left on the hearth. With my newfound love of tennis, I remember desperately wanting a new tennis racquet for Christmas. 'Well,' said my mother, 'I suppose if there is no Father Christmas there is no one to bring you that tennis racquet you want so badly.' To this day I recall lying in bed on Christmas Eve sobbing my heart out. When my mother asked, 'Darling what's wrong?', I replied through sobs, 'I do believe in Father Christmas, I really, really do believe in him.' And on Christmas morning there duly appeared a tennis racquet, and I have believed in Father Christmas ever since!

It was also at Kambala that my life-long love of ballet was born, and from a rather unlikely beginning. 'Twinkle' Blau was among my friends at Kambala. She and her family had come from Germany for her father to take up the management of the German company 4711 Eau de Cologne. Twinkle was having ballet lessons and I longed to do the same. I had visions of myself whirling around in a tutu and taking innumerable curtain calls while clutching large bouquets of flowers. As I was already

Me at home in Melbourne.

The Perry girls (*left to right*) –
Shirley, my mother Hilda and me.

having tennis lessons, my parents said I could not have both, so Twinkle volunteered to pass her knowledge on to me. We decided to give a performance at the school concert, and Twinkle and I assiduously practised our act, choreographed by her, in the school cloakroom. When the great night came, the curtain went up to the two of us on stage, in tutus courtesy of our parents. When the music started so did we. Unfortunately, the choreography went straight out the window. We each whirled around doing our 'own thing', at times narrowly avoiding collisions, and leaving four embarrassed parents in the audience.

Whether it was the ignominy of being associated with 'that' ballet performance, I do not know, but in 1931 my father accepted the offer from Hoyts to go to Perth to become state manager. In my youth, to travel to another state was enormously exciting as it meant travelling by ship. It was a momentous occasion with friends and family all coming to bid us farewell and throwing streamers to send us on our way. At this time, flying was still in its infancy and very expensive, and the only other alternative was a long and uncomfortable train journey crossing the Nullarbor Plain.

My mother, Hilda Perry.

My father, Stan Perry.

We set sail on the Adelaide Steamship vessel *Manunda*, which took about a week to sail between Sydney and Perth. Our days at sea were spent playing deck quoits, deck tennis, race games and all sorts of activities. At night, after dinner, when we young were tucked away in bed, the grown-ups danced – the men dressed in back tie for dinner and the ladies in long flowing evening gowns. It was all so glamorous to me. The three days crossing the Great Australian Bight, which is considered to be one of the roughest crossings in the world, was exciting, though thankfully to this day I have never crossed it when it was angry.

We settled in Perth, initially at Mount Lawley and later at Crawley, and Perth became my home for the rest of my unmarried life.

In Perth, my parents enrolled me at Perth College and my sister in the kindergarten. As well as sport and ballet, I had developed a new passion: horses. I read countless books about English girls' boarding schools, with their riding schools, hockey playing, and secret midnight feasts. It all sounded marvellous – especially as there seemed to be no mention of schoolwork! There was one school in Western Australia answering to this description: Kobeelya. Kobeelya was in Katanning, a town about 480 kilometres southwest of Perth. As I was not particularly happy at Perth College and my parents had heard good reports of Kobeelya and the school's advantages, they decided to enrol both my sister and me there. I was thrilled. Shirley was only six, but because of the age difference

Kobeelya, my school in Katanning.

between us, my parents believed we should be together while growing up. I can still remember Shirley on the train platform before we left for our new school. Se was clutching her teddy bear that was almost as big as she was, wearing her hat that was far too large for her little head, and with her much loved rag doll 'Sarah Jane' in pink rompers!

We arrived at Katanning in the early evening, where we were met by cars and driven to the school about three kilometres away on the hill overlooking the town. On our arrival, there was a meal awaiting us, after which we were shown to our dormitories and then to bed, although we were far too excited thinking about our new world to sleep! A local Aboriginal dialect word meaning peace, Kobeelya was built by Frederick Piesse, one of the earliest settlers in the area in 1902. After his death, the estate was broken up and the Church of England bought his house and twenty-one hectares of land for a girls' boarding school, which was officially opened by the Archbishop of Perth on 14 September 1922.

Kobeelya had its own farm that provided fresh milk, cream, eggs and vegetables for the school's kitchens each day. It also had a nine-hole golf course, horses and a riding school. Both my sister and I remember Kobeelya with the greatest of joy and affection.

Our daily routine meant rising at 7 am, washing, dressing, making our beds – I was forever being sent back to remake mine – breakfast, cleaning our teeth, then marching into the assembly hall for prayers before heading to our respective classrooms. Our mistresses, who all lived in, included a music teacher, a gym instructress, a history teacher, a geography teacher who also taught French, and Mrs Strugnell the headmistress who taught English. Mrs Strugnell was a wonderful teacher and although a strict disciplinarian, was a kindly woman. I have never forgotten being taught a personal lesson in English from her one day as she was walking through the courtyard when the bell was about to be to rung for the beginning of class. The bell was mounted on a stand in the courtyard and we all loved to go up to the stand and ring it. I asked Mrs Strugnell if I could do so and she said, 'Yes, June.' I ran to the bell stand and Mrs Strugnell said, 'June, where are you going?' 'To ring the bell,' I replied. 'Who gave you permission for that?' 'You did,' I responded. 'No, I did not. You asked if you *could* ring the bell, and I am sure you are quite capable of doing so, but you *may* not.' I have never forgotten that lesson! There was also the matron, a Miss Newham (known to us as 'Snew') and Miss Barter, the kindergarten teacher known as 'Barty'. In later years there was a domestic science teacher who taught cooking, budgeting, housekeeping and related topics. And all these teachers for only thirty girls!

Afternoons were divided between sport, lessons and homework, and then upstairs to wash, change into clean clothes, and come down properly dressed for dinner. After dinner in the summer, those of us in the riding school would be taken on twilight rides, and in the winter, Mrs Strugnell would often have small groups of us in to her sitting room at night to sit around her fireside and listen to classical music.

Weekends at Kobeelya seemed to fly by. On Saturday mornings, after breakfast, we went to the matron's office to collect our pocket money – sixpence for the junior girls and one shilling for the seniors. We would then proceed to the common room where a mistress presided over a large laundry basket of garments in need of repair, which included holes in stockings that needed darning and blouses without buttons that needed to be re-sewn. After collecting our articles requiring attention, we would sit there and do our repair work before presenting it to the mistress on duty for her approval, after which we were allowed to sign off.

Our mending satisfactorily completed, we would don hats and gloves and go down the hill to the village in threes or accompanied by a mistress. Our first stop was invariably the bakery for a pie or pasty with sauce, which we would eat there, as eating in the streets was strictly forbidden. Another favourite of ours was the sweet shop, where we could fill a bag of sweets for threepence. We often visited the haberdashery shop, where I would sometimes buy lace to sew on the edge of white cotton handkerchiefs to give to some unfortunate person for Christmas. Often there was also material to buy for sewing classes. My parents had opened an account at the local store, which I was only allowed to use for 'necessities'. Always very 'good' with money, I would buy things on the account such as Christmas presents for my parents from Shirley and myself and then tell Shirley what she owed me for her share of the present. She always seemed to have some pocket money left over, and she always paid up!

Despite the pies, pasties and sweets, we would return to school for lunch.

In the afternoon, there would be tennis, riding or golf, and on warm afternoons we would spread our rugs under the big pine trees and play my gramophone – I was the only girl who had one and was considered tremendously lucky. There were no portable radios or iPods then. Shirley says I had only one record, *The Girl in the Little Green Hat*, which I played incessantly. Sometimes on summer days we would go to Lake Maracoonda, where we would picnic in the bush around the lake. We would swim and ride on the flying fox across the lake, letting ourselves drop into the water.

Saturdays were also spent organising and practising the Saturday night entertainment. Each Saturday evening, a group of girls – either a dormitory or a group of friends – would be responsible for putting on an entertainment for the others, maybe a play or a game of some sort. Many imaginative ideas were thought up and we all had great fun. On weekends we would also have rehearsals for the annual end of year school play. On one occasion I played Titania in Shakespeare's *A Midsummer Night's Dream*. The day before my big performance I lay out sun baking all day. As a result, Titania was more 'nightmare' than 'dream' in floating blue chiffon and bright red skin with blisters!

With my love of sport, I was involved in all the sports played at Kobeelya, including tennis, netball and golf. I was named the junior champion athlete in 1932, and later the runner-up senior champion athlete. Golf was a particular favourite of mine, which had much to do with the afternoon tea we had afterwards in a little shed we referred to as the 'club house'. We would each contribute threepence weekly and one of us would be responsible for buying the afternoon tea. After a round of golf we would boil the billy, make tea, and picnic on the cakes and buns.

Before the summer holidays, a group of girls would be chosen for the choir to sing carols in the church at Mount Barker, about 100 kilometres south of Katanning, where the headmistress's husband, the Reverend Strugnell, was the Church of England rector. This was a much sought after event, mostly because of the high tea provided, and so only a select group of girls was chosen. Accompanied by a mistress, the group would leave Katanning by train in the morning and arrive at Mount Barker in time for a lunch provided by the local women. At 5 pm, we changed into out school summer dresses, made from white silk with lace-edged collars and short sleeves, and enjoy the long awaited high tea. Afterwards we donned blue organdie veils and, looking like little angels, walked slowly down the church aisle warbling carols. Once the service was completed, there were more refreshments, before we changed back into our school uniforms and boarded the train back to Katanning, returning rather tired from what was, to us, quite an adventure.

At the end of my schooling at Kobeelya, I stayed on for an extra year to attend the finishing class, which educated us in the skills of domestic science, social etiquette, and other such lessons considered to be of importance for a young woman in those days. One of our lessons was in deportment, taught by the gym instructress. This consisted of leaping gracefully into the air, pretending to catch pieces of fluff, and then landing lightly on the ground. Given the varying size and shape of the girls this would surely have made for an entertaining sight! We were also taught how to be presented at court and how to curtsey. This turned out to be not much use, for by the time my generation would have been presented, the war had started and there was no court at which to be presented. It was part of the custom in my day for girls leaving school to make their 'debut'. Some lucky ones would even be taken to England by their parents who would apply through Australia House to have their names put forward for a presentation ceremony there. At the presentation, girls wore beautiful long dresses – certainly *not* strapless – had their hair styled and wore long white kid gloves that came up over the elbow, known as 'court length'.

But the war signalled the end of the court, and another ceremony was relegated to the past. However, these lessons were to be extremely useful to me in the future when I was introduced to heads of state, governors-general, viceroys and royalty, when the occasional curtsey was expected.

Schooldays ended in 1935 and I looked forward to a life of parties and fun before, hopefully, marrying. My parents were then living at Crawley, close to the Swan River. The worst of the Depression had passed, but its effects were still evident. I had been sheltered growing up at Kobeelya, but I remember my mother saying that people frequently came to the door looking for jobs to be paid in food, not money.

Few of the girls whom I knew took jobs or went to university or even thought of a career. I had a short-lived desire to be a journalist and my father, who knew the editor of the *West Australian* newspaper, managed to find me a job as a film critic. I would go to see the latest films by myself and afterwards hand in my report. My report, however, was more plot summary than critique, and since I also did not enjoy sitting through the films on my own, my career as a journalist ended almost as soon as it began. But there was still much to keep me busy. My friends and I joined the Junior Victoria League. We organised parties for charity and assisted at the Lady Lawley Cottage By the Sea, a home for disabled children. We visited the home with gifts, took the children on outings, and conducted fundraising events on their behalf. My parents were wonderful role models in charity work. There was much family excitement when, on 11 May 1937, my father was awarded an Order of the British Empire (OBE) for his efforts in raising funds for a myriad of charities and causes.

My social life consisted of dances and parties. They were all quite formal and held in people's homes, so our parents knew where we were going and would always take us to and fro. On the occasions when I was asked by a young man to attend a ball, I would say to him, 'You'll have to ask my mother.' She would invariably say, 'Well, you'll have to ask her father.' After the young man had spoken to the three of us it's a wonder I was asked anywhere! But we had brilliant parties with lovely suppers and lots of dancing.

During this period, my friends and I also spent time on Cottesloe Beach and had crabbing parties on the Swan River beaches. When crabbing, two or three friends would walk ahead in the water with hurricane lanterns

and the rest of us behind with fishnets and buckets. The crabs would be attracted to the lights and we would scoop them into the buckets. On the shore, we would build a fire, cook our crabs, and enjoy them hot with fresh bread and butter and no doubt some beer as well.

Girls entering society, or 'coming out', routinely had their photograph taken by the popular social photographer at the time, Susan Watkins. There were unexpected ramifications when she took mine. The photographs were extremely good and my mother agreed for Miss Watkins to enter them in a competition, thinking it was a photographic competition since it involved the Crippled Children's Association for which I was fundraising. I was then asked to come to an interview by a panel of judges, and not thinking much of it, went along. The outcome, however, was that I was named Miss Western Australia. My mother was dismayed and my father furious – he imagined me being paraded around half naked in swimsuits. There was a terrible kerfuffle in our house, and the judging panel was informed that owing to illness I could not accept the honour nor attend the national final in the eastern states. The judges refused to give the title to the runner-up, so in 1937 there was no official Miss Western Australia. This did not prevent the *Albury Advertiser* basking in the honour:

> Katanning can consider itself honoured by the fact that the State representative of the Australia-wide campaign being run by Smith's Newspapers, for 'Miss Australia, 1937,' spent a considerable and important part of her life in Katanning. 'Miss West Australia' is Miss June Perry, who was for some years a pupil at Kobeelya, and a very popular one at that. Miss Perry was born in Melbourne in 1920 and attended St Michael's Church of England Girls' School, Melbourne, her education being completed at Kobeelya, where she was a champion athlete and a brilliant scholar.
> [*Albury Advertiser*, 4.3.1937]

Though I advanced no further in the quest, I entertained Miss Australia, Sheila Martin, when she went on her round-Australia trip.

Those photographs of me were obviously good, as recently I needed to replace the frame on one of them, and when I took it to the framer he looked at it and said, 'Oh, isn't she gorgeous,' and then looked at me and asked, 'Who is it?' I rather grumpily replied, 'Me.'

LEFT: One of the photographs taken by Susan Watkins that led me to being named Miss Western Australia.

CHAPTER 2

The Beginning of the War

War clouds were gathering over Europe, and a local branch of the Voluntary Aid Detachment (VAD) was started. I enrolled along with several friends. We received no pay but worked in military hospitals and did menial work to free trained nurses for more important jobs. We wore blue dresses with V-necks and white collars, a large white apron with a red cross emblazoned on the front and held with two wide straps crossing over at the back, and white veils. Black stockings and shoes completed the outfit. We felt like a bunch of Florence Nightingales!

We were given first aid lectures and taught to give injections by practising on oranges. I remember one night at a dinner party sitting next to a young man who had recently enlisted. He told me he was going to have his injections somewhere near Fremantle. 'Oh, we're giving injections there,' I told him. He said, 'Really, I didn't think you VADs gave injections.' I replied, 'Oh, yes we do. We've just started. We haven't given them to people yet, but we've been practising on oranges for weeks.' I think many a young man may have lost his enthusiasm for enlisting at the thought of an inexperienced VAD giving him his shots, believing it more frightening than going into battle!

Australia entered the war in 1939. I was having dinner at Pearce RAAF Base just outside Perth the night war was declared. I remember the silence as we listened to the Australian prime minister, Robert Menzies, saying Australia was now in a state of war with Germany. I looked around at all those fresh-faced young men and thought: 'I wonder how many of these will be here when all this is over,' and many of them were not. The first Australian soldiers went overseas in 1940 and RAAF pilots fought both overseas and also defended Darwin and New Guinea from the Japanese.

The night was also memorable for me for other reasons. I had been invited to the dinner by the tall and dashing Flight Lieutenant Brian

Me in the distinctive VAD uniform.

RIGHT: Invitation to the RAAF
Officers' Mess dance, 1940.

RAAF

The Commanding Officer and Members Officers' Mess
Royal Australian Air Force
PEARCE
request the pleasure of the company of

Mrs June Percy

at a

Dance

at the Officers' Mess, on Friday, 15th November,
1940, at 9 p.m.

R.S.V.P. 8/11/40
Secretary,
Officers' Mess

Dress

ENTRANCE TO STATION ONLY BY THIS CARD

'Blackjack' Walker (later Group Captain), whose commanding officer and wife were host and hostess.

Blackjack had some days earlier taken me for a flight (no doubt totally illegally) in his little two seater RAAF plane, and as we flew over my home in Crawley, he said, 'Would you like to loop the loop?' Of course my answer was probably, 'Can a duck swim?', so off we went! When I returned home my mother said, 'Some idiot has been trying to commit suicide over our house this afternoon!' When I told her it was me looping the loop she was aghast!

When Blackjack called to pick me up to take me to the dinner, he found that he also had my little sister along. My parents were not allowing me to go out to an airforce base among a lot of wild young men alone, even with the Commanding Officer and his wife hosting the dinner. So my younger sister was sent along, no doubt to keep an eye on me. I cannot imagine what would happen today if a young man called for his date and found that the little sister was also being sent along.

All of those young men around the table that night were to receive a distinguished Flying Cross or a DSO when the war was over and very sadly many of them were dead. Blackjack Walker's flying exploits became legendary. He was considered fearless and dedicated to flying and the science of flying. He led his squadron to victory in the battle of the Bismarck Sea, destroying the Japanese ships and convoys taking men and supplies to the Japanese fighting the Australians on the Markham River, with his squadron shooting down forty Japanese Zeros. After the war, Blackjack became the number one test pilot for De Havilland.

VADs were disappointed to be told that they, unlike their counterparts in England, would not be taken overseas, so I and two friends, Audrey Burt and Nan Clement, decided to become trained nurses, believing that if the war lasted we might still make it overseas. We enrolled as trainees at the Royal Perth Hospital, where I became known among my friends as 'Bedpan Perry'. Few girls I knew had jobs – least of all as nurses – so we were considered quite heroines among our friends. Our mothers embarrassed us by coming to the hospital and asking to see our rooms, and having done so, proceeded to provide us with new furnishings. Often when we came off duty, we would find a thermos of hot cocoa and biscuits left in our rooms.

My mother believed that my hair would fall out from wearing a nurses cap all day, even though the cap was minute and only sat lightly on the top of my head. She insisted that I have a 'hair-do' and a scalp massage every week. As we earned only ten shillings a week, with threepence deducted for the nurses' fund and sixpence for laundry, there wasn't much left for a 'hair-do'!

At the end of our first year of nursing, we all managed to pass at the top of our class before going into the wards. We had been nursing for only a few months when the government announced that VADs would now be taken overseas. We dashed along to enlist, thinking our extra training would make us more valuable. However, *because* of our extra training we were urgently required in Australia. The extraordinary issue with this policy was that if a woman married, she was not allowed to continue nursing training. One girl who started training with us secretly married when her fiancée returned from the Middle East. She was dismissed in disgrace when discovered. Soon afterwards, her husband was killed in New Guinea leaving her without a husband or a career. Happily things have changed today.

Audrey and Nan completed their nursing training and became first-class nurses. Chance conspired to steer me in another direction.

Since school I had continued my interest in riding and had become involved with the Western Australian Polo Club. Several players were friends of mine and I would often go to the grounds to help exercise the ponies. I tried playing polo, but learning to control the pony while wielding a mallet proved too much for me. In 1939 there was much excitement at the prospect of the South Australian Polo Team coming to Perth for the annual polo tournament. Apart from the polo, there were many social activities organised for the visit, including a ball at the Adelphi Hotel. Members of the South Australian team included Bill Hayward, later Sir Edward, who was accompanied by his wife Ursula; Donald Reid, whose mother Mrs Malcolm (Jean) Reid accompanied him; Ken Bakewell and his wife; and Tom Porter.

The morning the South Australian team arrived I had been in Perth shopping, and had bumped into Angus Maitland, a South Australian who was working and living in Perth. Angus introduced me to his companion Donald Reid. Later that same day I went to collect my father's car from

Watching one of the polo games at Hurlingham grounds, South Perth, 1939, with friends (*left to right*): —, Sue Bush, Marjorie Chapple, Tom Bush and me.

the garage where he left it each day. The garage attendant brought my car around just as Donald Reid and Tom Porter walked into the garage to hire a car for their stay in Perth. As I was leaving I waved and said 'Hello' to Donald, and as I glanced at the other young man, it was as though an electric shock went through me. As I drove off, Tom Porter, according to Donald, turned to him and said, 'Good heavens, where did you meet her?' As my nephew, James Porter, rightly said at my ninetieth birthday, 'At that moment such was the magnetism between them, that a spark was lit that never faltered in fifty years.'

When the tournament started at the Hurlingham grounds in South Perth, Tom sought me out and we were introduced. I cannot remember what we talked about, but I do remember my heart missing beats.

Tom Porter

Tom Porter was born on 10 July 1913, the son of stockbroker Frederick Windmill Porter and his wife, Clara Frances Porter. Tom was christened Robert Evelyn, but was always known as Tom. The story goes that Tom's grandfather had an old coachman called Tom, who had a little

Private Tom Porter, 1939.

red wizened-up face, and the first person to see what his mother thought was a beautiful baby said, 'Good heavens he looks exactly like Tom the coachman!' And the name stuck. Tom's father, with his grandfather – James Windmill Porter – had been a founding partner in James Marshall & Co, and when Myer acquired the business, his father remained as local director. Tom's father took a seat on the Adelaide Stock Exchange in 1929 and joined with Arthur Roy Taylor to form the sharebroking business Taylor & Porter. Tom had wanted to go on the land, to work on the property he owned with his brother James – known as 'Bun' – in South Australia's South East. When his father died on 4 October 1937, his brothers Bun and Arthur urged him to remain in Adelaide to represent family interests. So Tom took his father's seat on the Adelaide Stock Exchange in 1937 and established himself in business as the principal of the stockbroking business F.W. Porter & Co – although at that stage, Tom was virtually the only employee.

With the sporting and social demands on the visiting players for the few days they were in Perth, Tom and I had little time together. But at the polo ball, he told me that he was in love with me. Just moments before, however, I had been dancing with a young man and as the band paused to change to another tune we stopped dancing beside a group of chairs, where the daughter of one of the members of the Western Australian water polo team was sitting. Her parents had married rather late in life and brought this girl up in a very old-fashioned way. She was not very attractive, always dressed in very dowdy and old-fashioned clothes and always sat rather hunched up in a corner looking miserable. As I and my partner stopped near her, Tom Porter went up to her and said, 'What a very pretty dress you are wearing.' This girl looked up at him in amazement – no one had ever told her that before. I must say I was pretty amazed also! Tom then asked her to dance, which led to even more amazement as that had never happened before either. So she got to her feet and danced off with the most attractive man in the room looking absolutely stunned but radiant, the hunch appearing to have vanished off her back! Tom Porter then asked me to dance, told me he had fallen in love with me and wanted to spend the rest of his life with me. I thought, 'Well I have just heard you tell that wretched girl there how lovely she looks, so I didn't think it was a remark I could take very seriously, and certainly not after only one meeting!' However, being a romantic I'm sure I secretly thought how lovely if it were true. And I was to find out later that it was! I was also to find out that Tom's gesture toward that girl was 'pure Tom'. He saw her sitting there, a hunched-up and miserable wallflower, and just hoped to make her feel a little better. His kind and generous nature continued to reach out to people throughout his entire life.

Undaunted by my refusal to take his offer of marriage seriously, Tom asked me to come and visit him in Adelaide. Ursula and Bill Hayward and Mrs Reid had also invited me to visit them in Adelaide and I had already accepted the latter's invitation, so Tom urged me to come soon. This was easier said than done. Travel from Perth to Adelaide did not simply involve jumping on a plane as it does today. There was no daily flight service from Perth and seats were not always available at short notice. Furthermore, my parents did not permit me to go 'running around the countryside' with people they did not know. A letter from Mrs Reid confirming her invitation and saying that she was looking forward to welcoming me mollified my parents on that score. Still, organising a suitable time and arranging the plane travel seemed to me to be interminable! Tom's letters indicated that he was impatient to see me again, but Fate conspired against us. With the declaration of war, Tom had enlisted. He volunteered on 2 September 1939 and was called up on 15 November as a Private with the 2/10th infantry battalion in the Australian Imperial Forces (AIF). By the time I arrived in Adelaide, Tom was in camp in Ingleburn in New South Wales.

My flight to Adelaide was my first commercial flight. I had been taken on flights with Squadron Leader Brian 'Blackjack' Walker, strictly against regulations I'm sure, and had even looped the loop in his little two-seater air force plane. My flight to Adelaide took fourteen hours, and no sooner were we in the air before we had to land to refuel. The plane was very small compared with those today, and passengers were weighed as well as their luggage. I always felt that slim passengers should have been allowed a greater luggage allowance.

Phyllis Reid, the daughter of my gracious hostess, and I became good friends during my stay, and would remain so until the end of her life. Donald Reid, who later enlisted, came from his property in the South-East during my stay and dances and tennis parties were organised and I made many new friends who formed the basis of my friendships when I came to live in Adelaide after the war.

Tom was upset at not being there to see me and delegated his brother Arthur to 'look after' me. Arthur later told me that Tom had asked him to be sure to 'keep any wolves at bay'. So Arthur duly invited me out to dinner, and when he arrived to collect me informed me that we would be 'dining at home'. Home was *Cosford* in Gilberton, built in 1876 by their grandfather. It was a large and imposing Victorian mansion set on three hectares of land and comprising gardens, a tennis court, stables and horse yards, and large vegetable gardens. Arthur drove me through the wrought-iron gates up the drive to the house. We entered through a large entrance hall and into what was referred to as the 'smoke room'. Sitting in a large chair by the windows at the end of the room was Tom's mother.

Mrs Porter, previously Clara Frances Cudmore, had been a great beauty and was then a good-looking widow barely fifty years old. I was seated opposite her and offered a drink. She then proceeded to grill me until dinner was announced.

The dining room was large, with long windows looking out on to the tennis court and the old oak tree that was planted when the house was built. Mrs Porter sat at the head of the table. Behind her was a serving table, beside which stood a parlour maid in black dress, starched white apron and cap. The maid served dinner and then took her position beside the serving table and stayed there throughout the meal. Meanwhile, I, trembling like a aspen, continued to be grilled by my hostess. I sat there hoping that my training at home and school was coming to the fore and that my manners were passing muster.

Such is the strangeness of life and fate, because as I sat there trembling, little did I know that the very next time I entered that house I would do so as its mistress, and that it would be my home for over forty years.

From Adelaide I travelled on to Melbourne and Sydney to visit friends, before returning home to Perth in March 1940. It now seemed that Fate was keeping Tom and me apart. Tom was unable to get leave from Ingleburn Camp to come to Sydney while I was there, and so I did not see him again until May after he had received his commission as a Lieutenant on 1 March. Tom sailed from Sydney on 5 May 1940 aboard the troopship *Queen Mary*, which was taking the first Australian troops to England. The ship docked at Fremantle en route and during a brief shore leave, Tom and I spent a day together. He repeated his proposal of marriage but still I was hesitant, wondering if we might be caught up in the events of the moment. So Tom sailed away with nothing resolved between us, but once more leaving a fluttering heart behind.

The 7th Division AIF disembarked at Gourock on the Forth of Clyde, Scotland, on 18 June 1940, a fortnight after Allied troops were evacuated from the shores of Dunkirk. The Australians were sent south and camped on the Salisbury Plains, and as the Allies had barely escaped with their lives and were forced to leave their military equipment behind, the Australian Division was the only fully equipped division in England at that time. Tom had charge of a mortar platoon. He had mortars, but no vehicle to transport them. So, with characteristic Australian ingenuity, he commandeered a hearse and travelled around the countryside with his mortars tucked inside.

Two years after enlisting, after travelling to England, the siege of Tobruk, action in North Africa, Greece, Syria and Lebanon, appointment as Aide-de-Camp (ADC) to General Arthur Samuel 'Tubby' Allen on 21 October 1941, and numerous letters to me all looking like spaghetti after having suffered from the censor's scissors, I received a telephone call from Tom who was back in Adelaide. In January 1942, the 7th Division had been ordered to the Far East to bolster defences against the Japanese who had conquered much of South-East Asia after declaring war on the United States with the bombing of Pearl Harbor on 7 December 1941.

The Australian divisions from the Middle East were originally destined for the East Indies, but following the fall of Singapore in February 1942, Prime Minister John Curtin insisted the 7th Division return to Australia to reinforce mainland defences. Unbeknown to me, Tom had returned with the first Australian troops and had disembarked from the *Orcades* in Port Adelaide on 15 March 1942.

The 7th Division had embarked from the Middle East for Singapore and Tom

General 'Tubby' Allen and Tom returning to Australia aboard the *Orcades*, 1942.

with General Allen had flown ahead first to Calcutta, where General Allen conferred with his army chiefs and found it had been decided that Singapore could not be held, so his troops were diverted to Australia and Tom and General Allen joined them on the *Orcades* in Colombo.

So Fate had intervened once again. If I had been accepted to go overseas as a VAD as I had so dearly wanted, Tom and I would have passed mid-ocean.

It seemed that Fate also played a part in the perfect timing of Tom's call to me. I had just started holidays after my first year of nursing training and was free to visit him in Adelaide. In fact, I had already been attempting to get a train booking to enable me to spend my holiday in Adelaide with Phyllis Reid. But getting there seemed well nigh impossible! Following the fall of Singapore, the government was using all available transport for refugees or troop movements. But once again, Fate was on my side. My father was a good friend of Arthur 'Jack' Ellis, the Western Australian Commissioner of Railways, and asked him if there was any chance of my obtaining a berth on a train to Adelaide. On 20 March 1942, my twenty-third birthday, I had gone into Perth to do some shopping. While I was out, Jack Ellis rang my father to say there was a train going that evening to Adelaide, and he could, if I still wished to go, find me a place on it. My father rang my mother to find out where I was, and sent his secretary to find me and take me to the station where my mother met me with my suitcase, which I had already packed in anticipation.

The excitement of my departure was enhanced by the sudden appearance of my closest friend, Marjorie Chapple. In January 1942, Marjorie had become engaged to Charles Learmonth, a wing commander in the Royal Australian Air Force (RAAF), whom she and I had met two years earlier when he had been stationed at the Pearce Air Force Base. She had been trying to travel to Melbourne where Charles was on leave so they could be married. To this day I can still remember the pandemonium as all her family came running down the platform with her suitcase and clutching clothes they hadn't had time to pack. They flung Marjorie, her suitcase and her clothes on the train virtually as it was pulling out of the station.

All this came about because I had telephoned Marjorie to tell her about my leaving. She, in turn, had telephoned her father who had contacted

Jack Ellis who said, with what I imagine was frustration, 'Well, if those two girls don't mind sharing a berth, she can go too.' Marjorie, who had been washing her hair at the time didn't think twice. With wet hair and a sparsely packed suitcase she boarded the train with me. Once aboard, we collapsed in a heap in our carriage like two co-conspirators unable to believe our luck. I would not return to Perth for fourteen months.

After a hilarious three days crossing the desert, sleeping head-to-toe in one berth, Marjorie and I arrived at the Adelaide Railway Station. Tom and I managed to miss each other at the station because of a blackout, and believing that I had been abandoned, I rang the Reids who told me that a distraught Tom had just rung them to say that I was not on the train. The confusion sorted, Tom came dashing back to the station and we saw each other for the first time in two years – and in a blackout! Tom, Marjorie and I then went across the road to the South Australian Hotel to celebrate. We returned to the station to see Marjorie off to Melbourne, where she married Charles soon afterwards on 28 March 1942. Sadly Charles, who was decorated with the Distinguished Flying Cross and Bar for actions against the Japanese in March 1943 and promoted to Commanding Officer of 14 Squadron, was killed. He died courageously giving his life to save many others when his Beaufort bomber crashed into the sea off the northwest coast of Australia on 6 January 1944. The air base Learmonth was named in his honour.

After leaving Marjorie and driving to the Reid's where I was staying, Tom repeated his wish to share the rest of his life with me. But just as he did so, the taxi arrived at the Reid's house and everyone came running out to greet us, giving me no chance to reply. So Tom settled the matter himself. Early the next morning I had a telephone call from Tom, who said quite firmly, 'I have told my family we are getting married and sent a telegram to yours.' I never actually saw the telegram, but apparently when the local exchange rang my parents to say there was a telegram from Adelaide, my mother assumed it was from me saying that I had arrived safely, but when hearing the actual contents, fainted.

Although we were far removed from the bombings in Europe and later Japan, the war was still very real to us in Australia and impacted the course of our lives. There was a feeling of urgency, of having to live for the moment. Young people met and married and were almost immediately

parted when their husbands enlisted and were sent overseas. Every day we would hear that someone we loved, or knew, was killed, leaving young wives with children to care for alone. Yet in all the war years, I never heard anyone complain – there was a war going on and everyone was proud to play a part and look with hope to the future.

Tom and I married on 31 March 1942 in St Peter's College Chapel. Bun, Tom's elder brother, was the best man and Ian 'Hack' Hayward was the groomsman. My sister Shirley and Phyllis Reid were my bridesmaids. Since the poor harassed Jack Ellis was only able to procure one booking for the train trip from Perth to Adelaide for my parents, and neither would come without the other, Shirley, though still at school, was sent to be with me instead. I cried throughout the ceremony because my parents were not there, mopping my eyes with my veil so that it became damp and crumpled. Fortunately I was comforted through all this by the firm and loving handclasp of the bridegroom.

For my wedding dress, I found some ice-blue moiré curtain material. Rationing was in place so coupons were required for dress material. Phyllis Reid's dressmaker made me a beautiful, but simple, bridal gown,

LEFT AND ABOVE: Our wedding day, 31 March 1942.

My sister Shirley in our garden at Crawley, c. 1942.

with a pale blue tulle veil that was held in place with white gardenias. Short white kid gloves completed the bridal outfit. The bridesmaids wore pale blue chiffon dresses with ruffled necklines and sleeves. My father had asked Malcolm Reid if he would give me away in his absence, and my mother, through the affiliation of her club, the Karrakatta with the Queen Adelaide Club, arranged a wedding reception at the Club's North Terrace premises.

Following the reception, Tom and I left by train for Bordertown and thence for Childerley Park, Naracoorte, for our honeymoon. Childerley Park, named after a family property near Cambridge in England, was the farm jointly owned by Tom and Bun. Bun and his wife Patti and their baby daughter Patricia soon joined us. They had also figured prominently in the weekend celebrations. Tom had been asked to be godfather to Patricia, who was born while he was overseas, and Bun and Patti wanted to have her christened while Tom was at home. They asked Tom if he would arrange for Patricia's christening service when he went to book St Peter's College Chapel for our wedding. Accordingly, Tom asked a rather startled chaplain if he could book the chapel for a christening on 30 March and a wedding for the following day. This was 1942, and things were not done that way. Tom, however, explained the situation to the chaplain, and both christening and wedding proceeded as planned. Twenty-one years later we would take that little baby on an around-the-world trip with us, developing a great bond that remains to this day.

Tom had a week's leave after the wedding, and when he was not conferring with Bun on business and the running of Childerley Park, we took long horse rides around the property. Station hands were difficult to obtain during the war, so various jobs had to be done on the property while we were there. When Tom was asked to raddle some sheep, he asked me if I would sit in a hole in the fence of the sheep yard to prevent the sheep from escaping. I wore a battered looking driza-bone coat and a large old bushman's felt hat. It soon started to rain, and as the sheep milled around in the dusty yard, the dust became mud, and by the end, I was splattered from head to toe in mud. I sat there thinking to myself, 'Where was that glamorous honeymoon which I'd long imagined in the south of France, with me floating around in chiffon negligees?'

When we returned to Adelaide, Tom returned to duty with General Allen and I became what was known as a 'camp follower'. It was not easy to travel between states during the war with troop movements a priority. To travel from Adelaide to Melbourne, one needed to 'border hop' – this meant taking the train from Adelaide to Bordertown, being taken across the border by bus or car into Victoria, and then continuing the journey to Melbourne by train. This was difficult with luggage, but some wives managed it with children for the chance of a brief moment with their husbands while they were still in Australia before, perhaps, being sent to face the Japanese in New Guinea.

Australian headquarters were established in Brisbane. However, as General Allen was required in either Canberra or Melbourne frequently, I regularly engaged in 'border hopping' from state to state and stayed with friends, or, when possible, with Tom. It was a life of perpetual motion, but this was expected during the war. The *Australian Women's Weekly* of 20 June 1942 reported on my activities.

That decorative young person, Mrs Tom Porter, is now residing at Brisbane as her husband, Lieut. Porter, has been posted to a northern battle station . . . June is making Belle Vue Hotel her headquarters.

My friend Dibbie Ryrie from Sydney, whose husband Jim was in Tom's 2/10th Battalion, later joined me on my travels. At one stage, we heard that the Division was to be stationed near Brisbane, so we rented a corrugated iron house on a farm near Caboolture, north of Brisbane. Inside consisted of a linoleum square on a primitive kitchen floor, two bedrooms with iron-backed beds with saggy springs and lumpy mattresses, a couple of well worn-out chairs in the sitting room and, incongruously, a piano.

'Camp followers' – Dibbie Ryrie (LEFT) and me, 1942, in Caboolture, Queensland.

When the landlady discovered that neither of us played, she said, 'Well, I won't bother to lock it!' We moved in, and one morning awoke to find, to our surprise and delight, that during the night the army camp had been established virtually right around us. This meant that Jim and Tom could spend nights 'at home' with Dibbie and me.

Dibbie and I were both pregnant at this time, and I was violently sick every morning, leaving breakfast and morning chores to her. In the afternoon, we would walk about three kilometres carrying a billycan to fetch milk from the local dairyman, and as we walked home Dibbie would start to be sick on cue as we came to a large fallen branch of a tree, so I would take over preparing the dinner. It seemed to have been well organised between us. Dibbie eventually had a baby daughter, but I was not to have such a happy outcome.

Tom was soon on the move again. General Sir Thomas Blamey, Commander-in-Chief of Australian forces, had headquarters in Brisbane with General MacArthur, the United States' Commander. General Blamey came to inspect the 7th Division at Caboolture. Afterwards, he sent General Allen a signal: 'Request Captain Porter join my staff. Arrange onward movements immediately.' I remember it well, as Tom commented, 'Some request!' Tom did not wish to accept the appointment but as General Allen wisely advised, 'Refuse a posting by the Commander-in-Chief to his staff, say goodbye to your army career.' Tom reluctantly accepted the posting, and came to admire General Blamey enormously, later saying that Blamey had more moral courage than anyone he had ever known. Tom was promoted to Captain on 19 June 1942, and became ADC to Blamey on 7 August 1942.

General Blamey and General MacArthur then moved their head-quarters to Port Moresby, New Guinea, and Tom with them. As General Blamey travelled between New Guinea, Canberra and Melbourne, I left Brisbane and headed for Melbourne where I rented a dear little house in South Yarra and was able to spend time with Tom when he flew there

General Thomas Blamey with Tom in New Guinea, 1942.

With Tom when on leave
in Sydney, 1942.

With Tom when on leave in Melbourne, 1942.

with General Blamey. I had many friends in Melbourne, and among the older couples who had taken me, a young war bride, under their wing, was Doody and Ken Nial, who held prominent positions in Melbourne's social life. Ken was also Tom's second cousin. In another twist of Fate, he and his wife were to play a significant role in setting the seal on my journey to India.

About the time I moved to Melbourne, important decisions were being made far away concerning the government of the Indian province of Bengal, which would determine Tom's and my future. The role of the Governor of Bengal became a particularly important one when the Allies were fighting the Japanese in Burma immediately to the east, after they had been driven out of most of Asia. Lord Louis Mountbatten was made Commander-in-Chief in South-East Asia and moved his headquarters to Trinchomalee, frequently holding heads-of-staff meetings in Calcutta. The situation was complicated by the potential for civil unrest because of problems caused by the worst drought in living memory in Bengal, the ongoing conflict between Hindus and Muslims, and the rising tide of Indian nationalism promoted by Mohandas Karamchand Ghandi and his 'Quit India' movement. Englishman Sir John Herbert, had been Governor of Bengal until he took ill, and Sir Thomas Rutherford, Governor of the neighbouring province of Bihar, was asked to take his place temporarily until a replacement was appointed. Sir John Herbert died on 11 December 1943. British Prime Minister Winston Churchill appointed the Australian Richard Casey to be Governor of Bengal in November 1943 when it was evident that Herbert would not recover. Richard Casey, who had an American and a British ADC on his staff, requested an Australian ADC, and Tom was appointed the position.

Richard Gavin Gardiner Casey had already had a remarkable career. He had been born in Brisbane in 1890, the son of a wealthy company director. He attended Melbourne Grammar School, Melbourne University and completed a mechanical engineering degree at the University of Cambridge. He enlisted in the AIF during World War I, and served first at Gallipoli as orderly officer to Major-General Sir William Bridges, and later as a staff officer in France, where he rose to the rank of major and was awarded the Military Cross and Distinguished Service Order. Casey later joined the Commonwealth Public Service in 1924, acting as Australia's liaison officer in London. He returned to Australia after the accession of Scullin's Labor government, entering federal politics in 1931 as the member for the Victorian seat of Corio. He became Treasurer in 1935, and Prime Minister Robert Menzies appointed him Minister to the United States in 1940. In March 1942, soon after Curtin's Labor government assumed power in Australia, Winston Churchill offered him a position on the British War Cabinet as Minister of State in the Middle East based in Cairo. In this position he did excellent work quelling potential social unrest in Syria, Lebanon and Persia. A month after Casey was sworn in as Governor of Bengal on 22 January 1944, Tom was posted for 'special duties in India'. Casey's chief concern was to ensure the maintenance of civil order and to prevent any disruption to the Allies war against the Japanese. Tom's role was to accompany the Governor wherever he went and arrange his social and official diary.

Tom and I returned to stay with my parents in Perth while he awaited a ship to India. Here we met the very amusing Captain Hilary Hook and Captain Bernard Loraine-Smith. Hilary Hook was to become a close friend in Calcutta. He was a career officer in the British Army who joined the Deccan Horse, a cavalry regiment in India, and later served in New Guinea and Burma during the war. Hook and Loraine-Smith were in Perth awaiting transport to India with their regiments after working with Australian forces. We saw a great deal of them while in Perth, and they eventually sailed for India aboard the SS *Madura* with Tom on 20 April 1944. Bernard Loraine-Smith was later wounded in Burma and had a leg amputated, but this setback did not stop him from remaining a great huntsman and rider after the war.

Tom's appointment to Casey in Bengal seemed to have ended all hopes of our being able to enjoy brief moments together for the duration of the war. While my travel around Australia to see Tom had been complicated due to wartime conditions, travel to India or elsewhere in the world for a civilian woman seemed impossible.

CHAPTER 3

The Path to India

Having farewelled Tom on 20 April 1944, I became resigned to the idea that we would not see each another again before the war was over. During the war there was no travel outside Australia other than that of troops for official reasons, so my chances of joining Tom in India seemed hopeless. Still, I was comforted by the knowledge that Tom would not be in the direct firing line. But to my relief, Fate once again intervened in my favour.

After Tom's departure I returned to the eastern states to see his family, visit friends and do whatever war work I could since there was an ongoing requirement for voluntary helpers. While in Melbourne, Ken and Doody Nial invited me for drinks to meet Sir Thomas Rutherford, the Governor of the province of Bihar, and his wife Lady Rutherford, who were visiting from India after his role as acting Governor of Bengal. Sir Thomas Rutherford's wife, Audrey, was an Australian, born in Melbourne in July 1907. The daughter of Willie and Edith Dickenson, this petite and attractive redhead travelled to England as a young woman and there met the handsome young Scotsman Thomas Rutherford, a career officer and rising star in the Indian Civil Service. The two married at the British Embassy in Paris on 18 May 1926 and had lived in India since, though with annual visits to Australia. They were a delightful couple and fortunately took a great liking to me. They were most interested to hear about Tom in Calcutta with Richard Casey. Little did I know the importance this meeting would have on my and Tom's future.

I farewelled Victorian friends once more, and returned home to Perth. A short while later I received a cable from Tom saying that the Rutherfords were visiting Government House in Calcutta and had asked about me. He told them that I was at home chewing my finger-nails wondering how I could get to India. Lady Rutherford asked Tom if I would accept a position as her lady-in-waiting. She indicated that there would be no pay involved, but that I would be a fairly free agent to come and go as long as I spent a reasonable amount of time with her. I replied quickly with a mad comment like, 'Can a duck swim?!' My reply set the wheels in motion. The Rutherfords contacted Australian Prime Minister John Curtin and obtained authorisation for me to leave Australia. I then went about attaining a passport, the appropriate vaccinations and, most importantly, a place on a ship. Eventually I was notified that I had been allotted a berth on the SS *Glenartney* – a merchant ship of about 9795 tons built in 1940 for the Glen Line – that was leaving for Colombo on 20 September 1944. The delay in my learning of my journey and sailing meant the Adelaide newspaper *Truth* learned of my imminent travel to India and managed to capture my feelings exactly in an article they published on 26 August 1944.

> Give any young grass widow – in these days of eternal washing up and being washed out – a pair of seven league boots, Aladdin's lamp, a flying carpet, and a magic ring, and we'll guarantee she couldn't do any better for herself in the way of a beautiful dream than the situation in which Perth's June Perry now finds herself. Married to our dashing Tom Porter, AIF, she is now surrounded by the splendor of an Indian palace, for Tom is aide-de-camp to Governor Casey, of Bengal, and June has gone along.

Perth's *Sunday Times* of 27 August 1944 carried the same story under the heading 'Perth Girl Goes to India'.

> Reports state that Perth's erstwhile June Perry, daughter of Mr Stan Perry, OBE, and Mrs Perry, who married Adelaide's dashing and wealthy Tom Porter, of the AIF, on his return from the Middle East, is soon to be surrounded by the splendor of an Indian palace.
>
> Captain Porter has been appointed aide-de-camp to Governor Casey (former Australian politician) of Bengal, and Mrs Porter has gone along, too, to India.

I had no idea what to expect of India – in 1942 no one I knew had ever been there. Travel was not accessible like today, and pre-war travel from Australia was mostly confined to holidays in nearby Singapore or the 'Grand Tour' to England via Colombo, these places being the nearest one got to the East. To me India was a mystical and glamorous place, with the little knowledge I had formed from a diet of British history and literature from school, which included the writings of Rudyard Kipling and E.M. Forster. It was a world entirely different from the one I knew and I was eager to explore it. And as well as being a once-in-a-lifetime adventure, I would be closer to Tom.

The *Glenartney* was a merchant ship and so I was crowded into a cabin with four other women. There were four bunks, one on top of the other, and the fifth bed appeared to have been a converted seat. My fellow travellers included Carlotta Sinclair, Mrs Bennett, Miss Means and one other whose name now escapes me. The other women were older than me and three were also married. They were Americans travelling to rejoin their husbands in India who were working for the Standard Oil Company. They had been on leave and were returning to India before continuing to America. All were typical Yanks, but as the steward said, they were 'good sorts', and we all got along very well despite being crammed into the one cabin.

In my mad rush to leave I had not anticipated the effects of seasickness, and by lunchtime on the first day I was feeling worse for wear. I grew steadily worse during the afternoon but forced myself to go to dinner. Michael Steele, a friend in Perth, had told me prior to my departure, to 'carry on with ease and unconcern'. But as I wrote in my diary, 'This I've decided is all very well in theory but in practice a "washout"!' [8.9.1944] The following morning I decided against eating and instead enjoyed the sun on the deck all morning. In the afternoon I occupied myself with various card games. This became a regular routine.

Soon after we sailed we had a lifeboat drill where each of us was given a little 'panic bag' that contained a bottle of water, long-sleeved shirt, soft-brimmed hat, sunscreen, first aid kit and a penknife. For some unknown reason I added a bra to my kit, though how I thought I was going to change into a bra in a lifeboat while being targeted by Japanese and German submarines is now lost to the realms of history! We were expected to have our 'panic bags' and life jacket with us at all times, and during the trip several announcements came over the intercom telling us we would be sailing a zigzag course because of a submarine alert. As I lay in the sun on the deck using my life jacket as a pillow and looking out to the glassy seas, I found it hard to image that danger might be lurking beneath us.

Despite the many alerts, the trip was uneventful. On 15 September, our last night aboard, Carlotta Sinclair hosted a cocktail party to celebrate her wedding anniversary. Later, the men on board organised a party and we all finished up on the deck singing sea shanties into the breeze.

Life in Colombo

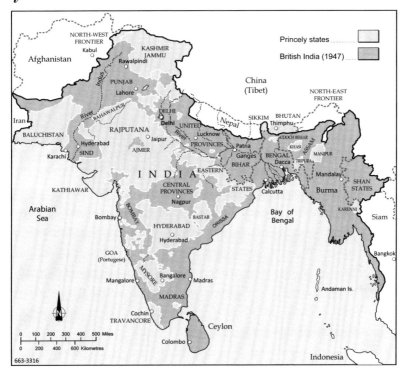

Map 1: India (Michael Ross).

The *Glenartney* arrived in Colombo on 16 September 1944.

> A marvellous sight. The Harbour simply crammed with ships that we wondered whether there was room for us! A large troopship was steaming out – mostly coloured troops aboard and two Dutch destroyers convoying it. It seems as though every flag imaginable is flying in the Harbour. Small craft are whizzing around the whole time and the whole place seems a hive of activity . . .   [Diary, 16.9.1944]

We anchored in the middle of the harbour and were told we couldn't go ashore that evening because transport was unavailable. I managed to go ashore in the agent's boat with Commander Gordon Fortune, a fellow passenger, to try to contact Tom's friends Doug and Dorothy Griffiths. A year before the war, Tom had been chosen to play rugby union with the Australian team that toured Ceylon, where he met and befriended another rugby player, Englishman Doug Griffiths, who headed a major shipping company in Colombo. Tom was to contact him in regard to my arrival in Colombo. After unsuccessful attempts to contact the Griffiths, I decided to have a look around Colombo despite the heavy rain at the time. We returned to the ship in the sanitary inspector's boat, which was not as unsavoury as it sounds, but Gordon did look slightly out of place in his number 10s uniform with masses of gold braid!

The next day I managed to contact the Griffiths only to learn that they had received no message from Tom, but they invited me to call on them anyway. I wrote of my trip to the Griffiths:

> Risked my life by going out to their home via taxi with native driver. He quite ignored trucks, cars, bikes, bodies – anything and everything that crossed his path. I arrived 10 years older, and 10 stone lighter from the sweat I'd broken into – and trying to look nonchalant! They insisted I stayed so back to ship for my clothes. In night went to film then Colombo Club and home for dinner ... Am trying to believe that a servant is actually drawing my bath and waiting on me most excellently. Fear I'll wake up in a moment and find it's Monday with washing to be done, dishes washed and floors to be polished!!   [Diary, 17.9.1944]

However, very soon I had become acclimatised to the traffic and wrote to my family back in Perth that

> I now sit back and relax, and take no notice of the things we 'almost' hit – it seems to be the 'done' thing here to miss death by inches every time you take to the road, so why worry?!   [Letter, 18.9.1944]

Despite my bravado, life in Colombo fascinated me. The weather wasn't very pleasant during my stay as it was monsoon season and there was a horrible dampness in the air. Every morning we rose late, breakfasted, shopped with a car and driver, had lunch, and then rested during the hottest part of the day. Most activities were taken in the late afternoon. This usually meant a round of social activities, including *thé dansant* (afternoon tea followed by dancing) at either the famous Colombo

Hotel, the Galle Face, or the Colombo Club. Then we would return home to change before going somewhere to dine and dance the night away. Coming from my rather sheltered life, I suffered severe culture shock.

> The place was full of spitting natives, which is dreadful. They chew Beetlenut and then when it's well masticated and full of spit they seem to cough it up, which looks just as though they're vomiting blood – very attractive! . . . Can't accustom myself to English method of speaking to natives. They are human beings although those crouched along the road look like animals really it makes me rather sad. The disorder everywhere is amazing and one wonders if anything can ever be done to rectify it . . .
> I think not. [Diary 18.9.1944]

The expatriates in Colombo took their life of luxury and social position for granted, and I was reminded of the Somerset Maugham remark made after having visited, that 'Having met the Memsahibs of the East, I now realise why there is such a servant problem in England!' I nearly burst one night when we were at the Colombo Club where a woman was complaining haughtily that her husband did not like going out for meals, and said 'I'm sick to death of ordering and eating meals at home.' I felt like asking her how she'd like to grill a chop every night of her life, eat it, and then wash the dishes after, but I refrained from doing so.

I left Colombo on 21 September, the Griffiths seeing me off at the airport. I had spent time at Thomas Cook's office trying to arrange my onward journey to Calcutta, finally managing to book a flight on a small six-seater plane to Madras – now Chennai – and then passage on the train across India. On the plane, the Anglo-Indian pilot began making passes at me. Seated directly behind him, he kept turning around and fondling my foot as I dozed off, which I endured only because he hinted that he might be able to arrange a flight from Madras to Calcutta for me which, as it turned out, he was unable to do, so my discomfort had all been for nothing!

We landed in Tiruchirappalli to clear customs, refuel and go to the toilet, there being no such facilities on the plane. There was also a little tin shed where we had sandwiches and a cup of tea as refreshments. The toilet was behind a little partition and consisted only of a bucket that went 'ping' when it was used, so everybody could hear. It was all highly embarrassing for a young girl fresh from Australia.

Crossing India

I finally arrived in Madras in the early afternoon and was met by the Australian consul and an agent from Thomas Cook who arranged to obtain bedding for me for the train trip to Calcutta (passengers had to take their own bedding whenever travelling overnight on a train in India). I was fortunate to have a school friend – Gweneth Peterson (née Edwards) – living in Madras, and so I surprised her with a visit. Gweneth's husband Ray was an architect working in the city. They had two small children and were living in Spencers Hotel, which was supposed to be the second best available but it was dreadful and shockingly expensive, but there was nothing else. A married couple worked for them as a nurse and a bearer, and on my way in I stepped over a rather unkempt servant lying across their front door, whom I discovered was their butler!

> Madras seemed an enormous city. I had a porter to help me take my luggage to the railway station and was most impressed with his ability to carry both a 'large case and bedding roll on his head and [a] small case by hand with greatest of ease.'   [Diary, 22.9.1944]

My few days in Colombo had been my introduction to the East, but nothing had prepared me for my arrival at the Madras Railway Station. The platform was a seething mass of bodies, with cripples lying or sitting all over the place and legless and deformed beggars with arms reaching out to grab me as I made my way to the carriage. Most were spitting betel juice, and there were masses of people cramming into the carriages and clinging to the outside of the train in the hope of getting a ride. I was quite shaken at this sight. But after a few days of travel I began to accept this as the way of life in India with its teeming population.

Trousers were not commonly worn by women at that time but I was glad that I had changed from my skirt to khaki trousers. I travelled on the Bengal-Nangpur railway and shared a carriage with two others – an English colonel's wife, and an Anglo-Indian girl, who worked in a Calcutta store. Equally interesting to me were the sights as we travelled across India. It seemed that every day was washing day in and about Madras, with dozens of people in the lakes and rivers washing their laundry on stone until it was clean and then laying it on the banks to dry.

The countryside was beautiful:

Everything is green now after the rains, and their [sic] are nice fields all along the way. At both sides of the track are swamps and waterlilies and water Hyacinths growing wild in them. Really beautiful. Every now and then you see a little Temple with a brightly coloured Frieze around the top of it, among the trees. The Indian villages are scattered along the way. Just huts with Palm leaf rooves – rather picturesque all nestling together.

[Letter, 25.9.1944]

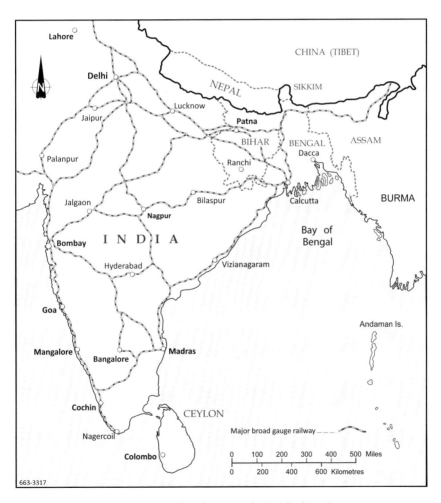

Map 2: Chief railway lines in India (Michael Ross).

I was interested to see pools of water everywhere, which contained lovely blue water hyacinths. I later learnt never to mention these flowers as they had been imported from Australia and had become one of India's greatest curses, blocking all the waterways.

There was no dining car on the train so we had to have our meals at the restaurants at the stations where the train pulled in. These restaurants were for first class travellers only and looked quite glamorous with white tablecloths and silver settings. The waiters looked most impressive too, dressed in lovely uniforms with white flared coats, white trousers, red cumberbunds and red turbans, usually with gold trimming. Our first meal was taken in the early evening. The restaurant looked wonderful, though reaching it meant passing further confronting scenes. In my diary I noted the stench of the station and the people all around, sleeping, spitting and relieving themselves in any way they felt like. The magic of the restaurant soon disappeared. As the servant put my bowl of soup down, I saw he had his finger dangling in the bowl. This put me off eating for the rest of the trip! In any case, most of the restaurants served only 'railway curry'. I was told that these were rather bland, as they could not include beef for fear of offending Hindus, nor pork lest the meal offend Muslims.

I did not sleep much during the three-day train journey. On the first morning we were woken early by people trying to enter the carriage – which was terrifying – thankfully the guards soon appeared to diffuse the situation. It was also difficult to sleep at night because of the din made by all the beggars and vendors at the stations through which we passed.

Everywhere people from tiny children to old men are jumping on the carriage door asking for 'Buckshees' or trying to sell something. One was selling fine toothcombs for de-lousing myself! He kept running it through his hair, and beard, then offering it to us to buy! Most attractive.

[Letter, 25.9.1944]

CHAPTER 4

Introduction to the Raj

During the time from 1767 to 1947, when Britain ruled the Subcontinent, India was considered the 'Jewel in the Crown of the British Empire'. British rule extended everywhere, even eastwards into Burma. There were provinces directly administered by the British, as well as the 'Princely States of India', which were ruled by Maharajahs who had a certain amount of autonomy, though each still had a British Resident. Governors were also appointed by Britain for each state, while state governments and bureaucrats were Indian.

In the early afternoon of Sunday 24 September I arrived in Calcutta, where Tom was waiting at the station to meet me. He had not told the Rutherfords of the exact date of my arrival so we could spend some time together. It was hard to explain our joy at being together again and our astonishment that it could have happened. From then on I was constantly amazed at the life I was living, my existence became one of privilege as I became a small part of the system of the Raj.

My first experience of the power and prestige of the Raj was at the station when the Government House car drove down the platform to the carriage enabling me simply to step from the train straight into the car. On a later occasion when I was returning to Bihar after visiting Calcutta, Tom took me to the train and remained talking to me through the carriage window while waiting for the train to leave. We wondered about the delay after departure time had passed. Eventually the stationmaster approached Tom and asked if he could start the train. Tom said, 'I can't do it. I thought that was your job?' I remember the stationmaster replying, 'But sir, we are waiting for you to finish your conversation. Have you finished your conversation?'

Tom took me directly from the station to Government House, which had been built as a palace for the viceroys by Lord Wellesley in 1799, when Calcutta was the Indian capital before Delhi. The building was

Aerial view of Government House, Calcutta.

designed on a grand scale similar to *Keddleston Hall*, the Curzon family home in Derbyshire. Prior to this, governors had resided at *Bukimham House* located on the same site. The compound was eleven hectares in area and the house comprised sixty rooms, including the Throne Room, which was used for receptions and contained the thrones of Lord Wellesley and Tupu Sultan. Government House featured an enormous main central portion with four wings leading from it and contained bedroom suites, all named after former viceroys. This imposing palace and the Bihar Government Houses at Patna and Ranchi, were to be my homes for the next fourteen months.

We drove through the ornate gates of Government House and followed the driveway to a large pillared portico. Guards stood on either side of the entrance, which opened on to a marble hall. I was ushered in to what I believe was the Curzon suite, overlooking the swimming pool and garden. I had a large bedroom with a canopied bed, as well as a sitting room and bathroom. It was beautifully furnished with contemporary materials and

Young Don Casey with his miniature electric powered car and instructor,
Government House, Calcutta, 1944.

furnishings, mostly brocades. Government House was basically a palace,
and by anyone's standards was extremely grand. I could not believe my
circumstances.

> It seems hard to believe that it's me – here with T[om] installed at
> [Government House]. All seems most odd. I've so much to say that I
> hardly know where to begin. Firstly Tom looks really marvellous. He's
> put on a bit of weight, which suits him more, and he looks really fitter
> than he has for some time – must say he seems pretty pleased to have me
> here!!
> [Letter, 25.9.1944]

I found the service that I received to be as grand as the surroundings.
Tom and I lunched in our room that first day and were waited on by no
less than four servants. The servants were dressed in 'white breeches and
coats with flared skirts a' la Arabian nights!'. [Diary, 24.9.1944] Whenever
I stepped out of my room about six servants jumped to attention and

saluted. And when waiting on table, they wore white cotton gloves, which I appreciated after my experience on the train from Madras.

After a leisurely afternoon by the swimming pool, we dressed and went to the ADC's room, where Tom had arranged to introduce me to several of his friends. The ADC's sitting room was in the lower section of Government House where, during the war, big concrete pillars had been built to give it extra strength in the event of air raids – we dubbed it the 'Paris Underground'. Many of those present to welcome me that first night became particular friends of Tom and mine. These included Casey's secretary Ernest Porter (dubbed 'My Goodness' by Casey, while Tom Porter was 'My Guinness'); Lawrence Pratt, a British Army officer; Colonel McPherson; Colonel Rex Peel, the military secretary; Ed Greever, a fighter pilot and the new American ADC; Peter Carr the English ADC; and a most colourful character named Boris Lissanevitch, about whom many books have since been written.

Boris was a white Russian born in Odessa in 1905. He was wounded in the Russian Revolution and later became a dancer with Diaghilev's Ballet. In 1924 he defected while in Paris and came to Calcutta sometime in the mid-1930s where, with the support of a consortium of maharajahs, he established Club 300 in December 1936 – modelling it on the exclusive and famed Club 400 in London. Club 300 became the favourite haunt of expatriates, Indian royalty, socialites and senior personnel, and now Tom and me.

The ADC room in Government House was a particularly social place and the centre of a network of expatriates in Calcutta. Security did not seem to have been much of an issue despite the war, and there was a constant stream of military and civilian visitors, many of whom were invited to enjoy use of the Government House tennis courts, swimming pool and its hospitality generally.

We assembled before dinner for drinks in the Yellow Drawing Room – so called because all the chairs were covered in canary yellow linen. This was a long room with a marble floor, with ornaments and paintings everywhere. I met Richard Casey for the first time at dinner. Mrs Casey was ill with a fever, so there was only Casey, Peter Carr, Pat Jarrett, Tom and myself. Pat Jarrett was an interesting person. I learnt that she had been a champion Australian sportswoman and international

RIGHT: Tom in the ADC's room, Government House, Calcutta, 1944.

BELOW RIGHT: Peter Carr, ADC, Government House, Calcutta, 1944.

BELOW: Staff of Government House, Calcutta, photographed by Cecil Beaton. Includes far left Richard Casey, third left Viscount Lord Pollington (later Earl of Mexborough), sixth left Noel Coward, far right Tom, fifth right Maie Casey, fourth right Pat Jarrett, 1944.

cricketer, and afterwards became a sports journalist and when she met Richard Casey became his press agent. But with the outbreak of war, she returned to Australia as a war correspondent, later agreeing to become Maie Casey's secretary after the Caseys moved to Bengal, joining them on 4 March 1944.

I sat on Richard Casey's right during dinner and had a wonderful time. I found him very charming. He asked me to go and see Mrs Casey the next day. Mrs Casey was ill in bed with dengue fever, but was still a most charming and pleasant woman.

Those first few days in Calcutta were eye opening. With the use of a Government House car and driver, I ventured into the markets and shops. The little streets leading up to the market were lined with small shops containing goods of all descriptions and I found myself besieged by the owners trying to drag me in. The market was a large covered area and a simply dazzling sight, containing dozens of stalls with brightly coloured cotton saris, and others with silk saris stacked on tables. Hanging from above was brassware of every description, metal cooking pots, ropes of coloured beads, a myriad of glass bracelets, and bright bedding covers. Around all this could be spotted a snake-charmer as well as the odd monkey – certainly different from shopping at home! One place that sold only cottons simply amazed me. After having experienced the empty shops in Australia because of rationing there were so many things to buy and they were all so gorgeous. I had already become aware of the need for many changes of clothes – it was frightfully hot and within five minutes my clothes were completely wet through with perspiration.

I looked at everything in wonder, trying to understand something of the people and culture of this country, which was now my home.

While the market fascinated me, everything around me seemed to become dirtier and dirtier as we ventured further into town. The streets were literally running with filth and unbelievably smelly. There were people everywhere and rickshaws carrying people or laden with goods, sometimes almost overflowing, but with skilful operators who could weave in and out of the crowds and the wandering cows. Considered sacred by the Hindus, cattle were free to wander through the town and into shops and no one could touch them. Tom had even seen a cow giving birth on the street and no one took much notice of it. There were people squatting by the side of the road, cooking their meals in round metal pots on burning cow dung that let off a pungent smell and sent up a cloud of smoke that created a haze in the air. Women in brightly coloured saris carrying baskets on their heads walked gracefully through the crowds. There were people lying in the streets day and night, passers-by simply having to step over them. I was fascinated by this very different way of life, so foreign to me. I became quite adventurous and at one point got lost down a dubious-looking street and had a monkey jump on my skirt and cling there for some time.

I believed it best to wait to become more adjusted before buying too much in the way of clothing, as initially it was all so overwhelming. I did, however, embrace the local way of having someone come into the palace and give me a fitting for some dresses.

> It seems too silly, ordering a frock and demanding delivery in a day, & the dressmaker coming to give the fitting – none of this rushing to them – you make your own time for them to come. It's most amusing to me.   [Letter, 25.9.1944]

I also had a much needed 'hair do' at a rather grubby salon managed by the equally grubby-looking girlfriend of the Maharajah of Cooch Behar.

Lunches and dinners at Government House were mostly spent in distinguished company, and one day I found myself the only female at lunch with Sir Asoka Roy, the law member of the Viceroy's Council, the Prince of Berar and Major-General Eledross. If I have been accused later in life of being a 'good talker', I can say that my skills were well and truly honed from the moment I set foot in India. I was now making conversation with people from all walks of life – from an Indian prince to a British major-general to highly ranked government officials as well as members of the household staff.

That first week was particularly hectic. Tom and I had fun poking around the markets, and lunched at the Saturday Club with Lawrence Pratt, where I met young Robin Sinclair of the Royal Air Force (RAF), a son of Sir Archibald Sinclair, a wealthy landowner from the north of Scotland who served as Liberal leader from 1935–1945 and as Air Minister in Churchill's ministry during World War II. We visited Robin after the war in England and stayed with him at his Scottish castle. Not long after my arrival, Boris hosted a dinner party at his Club 300 attended by Pat Jarrett, Lawrence Pratt, Tom, and me. The dinner consisted of four women and ten men, which I came to appreciate was the usual gender balance wherever one went. The upside of this was that the women were well looked after. I was intrigued to find that I wrote of the night in a letter home to my family: 'Marvellous dinner – soup, snipe stuffed with chickens liver and brandy, and a rum omelette to finish with, which when one cut into it was stuffed with bananas and grapes.' [Letter, 25.9.1944]

Tom also introduced me to Tolly Gunge, the golf and racing club. Tolly Gunge had been established in 1895 as an equestrian and sports facility of forty hectares, members entering through the 200-year-old clubhouse out onto sweeping lawns. It was a wonderful place – a big old country club with beautifully manicured lawns dotted with tables with umbrellas. I remember sitting there and seeing one of the servants bring out afternoon tea on a big tray laden with interesting morsels. Either side of the servant was another servant waving a flag above to frighten away any crows before they whipped the food away. We sat outdoors and had iced coffee before returning home. The ADCs had their own jeep, which was grand, but I nearly fell out of it a dozen times during the ride to Tolly Gunge and back!

Introduction to Indian royalty

My introduction to Indian royalty came after I had been in Calcutta for only four days. Tom and I went to visit Jagaddipendra Narayan – known more familiarly as Bhaiya, Maharajah of Cooch Behar, a territory in North Bengal in the foothills of the eastern Himalayas. Bhaiya was born in 1915, and so was only a little older than me. His father had died in December 1922, which meant he became Maharajah of Cooch Behar when he was only seven years old, with his mother acting as regent. He was educated primarily in England at St Cyprian's School, Eastbourne, then Harrow and Trinity College, Cambridge, before graduating from the Prince of Wales Royal Indian Military College. He served in the British Army during World War II in North Africa, Assam, Burma and South-East Asia.

Bhaiya was one of about 600 rulers of royal states that together

Tolly Gunge racetrack, Calcutta, c. 1944.   With Bhaiya, the Maharajah of Cooch Behar, 1944.

comprised about forty per cent of India's territory. These Maharajahs ruled their royal states directly in accordance with treaties negotiated with the British government – a British Resident in each royal state acted as a liaison between the princely state and the government in Delhi. The relationship with people of the state was essentially a feudal one. Other states were under direct British rule and were collectively known as British India.

Bhaiya visited Calcutta regularly, during which time he lived in the large family residence *Woodlands*. The Cooch Behar family had turned *Woodlands* over to the government for use as a hospital at the outbreak of the war, maintaining only a small section for use as a home when in Calcutta. Bhaiya and Tom had become friends because of their mutual interest in horses and their comparable service in North Africa. In fact, Tom had joined friends Bhaiya and Boris Lissanevitch in partnership with two horses that they raced at Tolly Gunge. The horses were named Crowpark and Double Brew. Boris had a gap between his front teeth and he could not pronounce his r's, so called the horses 'Clowpak' and 'Double Blue'. When Bhaiya heard I was to visit India, he asked Tom to bring me to Cooch Behar as soon as I arrived, and Tom organised his leave for the weekend to do so. We arrived at Cooch Behar early on Friday morning after travelling overnight by train.

Bhaiya – the Maharajah of Cooch Behar – in a formal portrait.

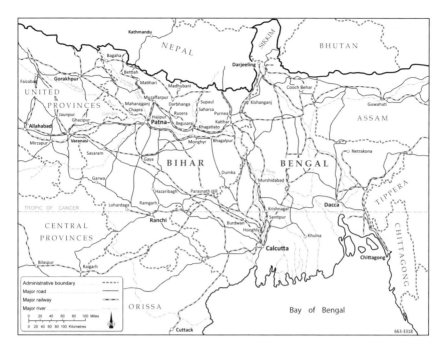

MAP 3: Bengal and Bihar States, India (Michael Ross).

> Bhaiya (pronounced 'Bie-ya') met us at the Station and drove us off to the
> Palace here – en route all the villagers who saw the car coming dropped
> their bundles and fell flat, bowed, or saluted – then as we drove in the
> Palace Gates the Guard sprang to attention & the Bugler played a clarion
> call! (This happens every time he goes in and out.)   [Letter 1.10.1944]

The Maharajah's car was meant to proceed at a stately pace along
the drive to arrive at the front door as the anthem stopped when the
Maharajah would alight from the car. But Bhaiya had a passion for fast
cars and whenever he was driving he accelerated through the gate and
along the drive to try to beat the bugler who also accelerated his fanfare.
Bhaiya was never able to beat him!

The long drive from the gates to the palace was totally bereft of trees.
The Maharani of Cooch Behar, Bhaiya's mother, had removed them as
part of her *puja*, or repentance, for the liberated life she had led and in
accordance with what she believed were the gods' wishes. The Maharani,
who was affectionately known as 'Ma' Cooch Behar to friends and family,
was an extremely beautiful woman and had been well known in the

social circles of Europe as a great hostess who gave lavish parties that were the talk of the town. She had also been the leader of the emancipation of Indian women. In her later life she had some feelings of guilt about the life she had led and had turned to prayer.

I immediately warmed to Bhaiya and found him a great deal of fun. He was tall and good-looking and spoke perfect English. This was the first time I had met Indian royalty and it was hard to believe that I was with a King in such a relaxed and informal atmosphere. We all teased Bhaiya and even ordered him around on occasions. But when he was with his subjects on official occasions, he was every inch the King, and it was clear that his people and his servants adored him.

The state was bankrupt when Bhaiya completely took over when he turned eighteen. His father died after squandering the fortune, or most of it, and all Bhaiya had to inherit when he came of age, were debts. He was only twenty-eight when we met him, and already he had paid the state's debts and begun to show a profit.

The town of Cooch Behar was charming. The houses were built mostly from bamboo and thatch and perched on stilts to protect them from the floods, with hibiscus plumes covering the rooves. At the centre of the town was a lake surrounded by white painted state offices. Little white temples were surrounded by gardens, and palm trees were dotted around everywhere and lined the red gravel road. The palace was situated some distance from the town. It was a colossal brick building designed by an English architect in 1870; long and thin, it had wings extending from either side of the central entrance hall. It had wide verandahs on each side providing protection from the sun, and punkers – strips of material connected to ropes used to 'stir' the air – in the main rooms during the summer heat.

The palace was decorated lavishly with brocades on the walls that could be easily taken down in winter. I wrote of our luxurious stay:

> We alone have 4 rooms – and there are 10 others staying here, all with pretty much the same space – and all together we don't take up half one wing. I believe there are thirty-six staircases in the place, so that will give you some idea of its size. Our rooms have hand painted walls – tiny flowers all over them to match the colour scheme of each . . . All this

ABOVE: Palace of the Maharajah of Cooch Behar, 1944.

RIGHT: Front gates to the Palace of the Maharajah of Cooch Behar, 1944.

opens out onto our own terrace . . . The throne room has a marble floor, and patterned in blue and white as are the walls and ceiling. The throne is mounted on a marble platform, and is all silver with two Silver Tigers pulling it. There is a proper Military Guard of his own Army, everywhere. They change every two hours, and it's quite a performance. The Court Artist is painting the Palace for us, so you'll be able to see what it's like. [Letter, 1.10.1944]

Tom also described the palace in a letter written home to his mother:

The palace is very large and some of the things they have in it are priceless. One room has the walls completely covered in Brocade. It's taken down in the Monsoon weather. It fits on with press-studs and looks beautiful a dull pink. Carpets threaded with gold and silver and large marble tables with every imaginable colour in it. Silver ornaments of every description and masses of cups and trophies for polo and racing. They have a huge Library with every conceivable book but not many novels mainly History, Biography etc. Most of the furniture is lacquered and I liked it. June didn't. One was completely Chinese and all the others varied in colour. [Letter, 5.10.1944]

On our arrival we had lunch and afterwards went on a tiger shoot, most definitely another first for me though not for Tom. Cooch Behar was the most famous 'shoot' in India and was visited by the most important people and the crowned heads of Europe. As early as the eighteenth century it was common practice for the maharajahs to arrange shoots for their guests in their jungles in which tiger, leopard, rhino, bison and samburh (a type of deer) roamed. These wild animals often caused disruption to local farmers by killing domestic animals used for their livelihood. Bhaiya had a wonderful team of elephants. Bhaiya's grandfather, the Maharajah, considered a line of less than forty elephants to be no good in the jungles throughout which he shot.

Capt. Viscount Pollington and me with a large sambar shot on a mixed beat, October, 1944.

Preparing for a tiger shoot, Cooch Behar, 1944.

On our way to the tiger shoot – John McDonald, US Consul in Calcutta, and me.

It was considered a great honour to be invited on a shoot by one of these rich maharajahs. The shoots were highly organised affairs requiring elephants and their *mahouts*, hundreds of locals to act as beaters, and then the journey to the destination where it was reported a tiger or leopard had made a kill, which often meant going across streams. The shooters and supplies for the shoot would be taken across on bamboo rafts and the elephants swam. Everything was then reassembled. The beaters would start beating and walking towards the shooters who were all arranged in a slight semi-circle. The beaters knew that the main shooter – whether the maharajah, the governor, or a special guest – would be in the centre and would try and drive the animal towards them. They would use saucepans or anything that made noise, as well as screaming and yelling. There was no real etiquette as to who had first shot, simply the person who was closest or saw it first.

The Cooch Behar jungles had few natural forests and were mostly made up of heavy grass, reed, patches of brushwood, and sal trees. The state was divided into small farms, the buildings encircled by groves of plantain, bamboo and other quick-growing trees. These homestead farms were one of the principal features of the country. For this particular shoot

Doris Driver and me with a leopard after the shoot.

Boris Lissanevitch and George Singh with leopard. 'Bag': one Russian, one leopard.

Tom with leopard after the shoot.

we drove about five kilometres to a delightful spot on the jungle's edge. It was amazing to step on the elephant's trunk and then be lifted up and put on its back. We rode in a *machan*: a type of box on the elephant's back that had a seat in it. En route we came across an amazing sight – hundreds of vultures were gathering around a cow that had been killed by a leopard. We went in search of the leopard. Riding through the jungle I wondered how on earth we were going to travel through it, but the elephants simply cleared a path, flattening any tree that was in their way.

> Beaters go ahead on Elephants to get it [the leopard] from under cover and then as it rushes out those with guns shoot. We were among the Beaters (the girls that is) and Tom etc shot. It was an enormous one and they got it pretty quickly. It made a rush at one Elephant, clawing its side and taking quite a hunk out of its ear. The Elephant never moved – just stood its ground and the Leopard was shot before anything else exciting could happen.
>
> [Letter, 1.10.1944]

Coming home the fireflies were everywhere. They looked like jewels shining in the dark. It was close to midnight before we dined, afterwards playing records and generally messing about.

We spent part of our visit walking about the palace and exploring the grounds, in particular the doll's house, which was a renowned feature.

Sydney de Kantzow.

Later we were joined by Angela May, the sister of Bhaiya's girlfriend Joan May, and Sydney de Kantzow.

Syd de Kantzow was something of a legend. He was an Australian who had served in the RAAF, but now flew for the China National Aviation Corporation (CNAC) from 1940 to 1945 (the CNAC had been established in 1929 to inaugurate commercial aviation in China and had been taken over by Pan American Airlines in 1933). Syd was originally based in Hong Kong until it fell to the Japanese, then in Burma until it was overrun, and then finally India.

The importance of the war and the advance of the armies in Europe somewhat overshadowed the importance of what was happening in South-East Asia and the strategic and political importance of Calcutta. The frequent presence of Lord Louis Mountbatten, the Commander in Chief of South-East Asia, and all his heads of staff conducting meetings at Government House, in conjunction with the many Allied troops in the area, meant that the war seemed very close. The Japanese were advancing along the borders of Burma and India. Calcutta was the staging area for B29 Superfortresses, which flew from the area to attack targets in Singapore. General Orde Wingate formed 'The Chindits', a remarkable force of men who made deep airborne penetration and fought behind enemy lines. It was the largest Allied special forces division of the war.

The Burma Road having been blocked by the Japanese in 1942 and Burma having lost its remaining supply line, the troops there relied solely upon airdrops for supplies. Flying in and out from Calcutta were the military transports supplying China's war effort. This flight was from Calcutta to Kunming in China, over what was know as 'the Hump' – an extremely dangerous route over high mountains and deep gorges with no reliable charts or radio navigational aids and little weather information. Pilots flew round trips daily despite these conditions, making this the first sustained long-range, around-the-clock, all-weather military aerial supply line in history. Over forty-two months, 650,000 tons of material was delivered. 'The hump' pilots frequented Government House in Calcutta, Syd among them.

Syd was the only person with whom Madame Chiang Kai-Shek would fly. It was said that on one occasion when flying over the Hump with Chiang Kai-Shek, Syd was warned that a Japanese plane was just above him, so with no time to warn his passengers, he took a dive and weaved in and out of the mountains, eventually reaching safety on the other side, He said that the only thing he lost was Madame Chiang Kai-Shek's lunch!

Syd was well known and liked by the Caseys because he had taught Richard and Maie Casey to fly in Australia before the war. The Caseys had managed to have him released from jail after he had a problem with the Chinese, and he became a regular visitor at Government House in Calcutta. Syd also taught Bhaiya to fly.

Tom and I had a certain amount of free time during our visit but

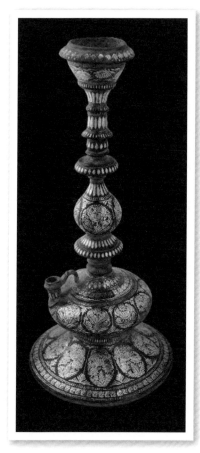

The Bidri hookah.

still had to observe some formalities. Drinks were served in Bhaiya's sitting room, lunches later in the afternoon to permit a sleep until early evening, and then evening drinks in the upstairs drawing room before dinner was served.

Our visit to Cooch Behar coincided with the time of the year when all the tenant farmers came to do *pujahs* and pay their respects to their Maharajah. One of the ceremonials included approaching the Maharajah, who was seated cross-legged on his throne, and each in turn would approach and smoke the hookah pipe with him. Bhaiya would return to us after these ceremonies, each time complaining bitterly about having to smoke the pipe, which he did not like at all. One night after the usual very jolly and late dinner we were all in the billiard room and the hookah wallah was sitting in the corner with the pipe. Tom said to Bhaiya, 'What on earth is all this that you keep complaining about?' and went over and started to smoke the pipe. Shortly after he said 'Aren't those pink and blue bubbles floating over the table simply beautiful?' No one else in the room could see any bubbles, but he kept insisting that there were more and more floating around, and all such gorgeous colours. He later said to me, 'I can tell you there is more than water in that pipe!' Happily that was his first and last experience with opium!

On the Saturday night we danced on the terrace after dinner and at about 4 am we decided to go jackal shooting. Those who went included Bhaiya, Tom, me, John McDonald – the American Consul in Calcutta – Ben Driver and his wife Doris, Syd de Kantzow, and Sylvia Clarke, the wife of another pilot. Tom and Syd did the shooting with the aid of the car's light, and Bhaiya drove. At the polo field we shot a jackal after much rushing about, and then chased for about another hour or so before going after two foxes. In his enthusiasm, Bhaiya drove into a swamp and bogged the car, which meant we had to walk back to the palace. I remember returning – by this stage we were a bedraggled lot and with the women still in evening dresses – and the guards did not recognise us, even challenging us at the gates. I had only been in India a week and was still feeling like Alice in Wonderland. Being with a king and being with him while being challenged by his guards at his palace gates had not previously come into my equation!

We rose late the next morning and played skittles in the billiard room. Later in the day we went on another shoot, but this time saw nothing but jungle, which I found rather beautiful. That day we also saw the elephants being washed and the mothers washing the baby elephants. There were two little fellows each about two years old who

Elephants being washed, Bihar, 1944.

made more noise than all the others. They were christened that day, one 'Syd Presenda' and the other 'Ben Bahardus', after Syd de Kantzow and Ben Driver. The elephants were absolutely marvellous and knew every word the *mahout* said to them. I felt I was on a magic carpet ride seeing one remarkable scene after another.

We went to bed early the night before we were due to leave, but not before 'Tom took swig of petrol thinking it was vodka and from then on

operated on about ten cylinders!' [Diary, 1.10.1944] On reflection, this probably led to his unsettled night. With Tom being something of a sleep-
walker, that night I woke to find Tom trying to get out of our canopied
bed, which had mosquito netting all over it. I thought he was simply
going to the bathroom, and when I asked him where he was going, he
responded, 'I'll be back in a minute. I'm going to the bathroom.' When
he did not return as promised I went to look for him and realised he was
sleepwalking. There were two guards at the top and bottom of each of
the staircases, but as I had been in India barely one week, the only word
I knew in Hindi was *sahib*. I went up to all the guards at each staircase
saying, 'Have you seen *sahib* in white pyjamas?' They just grunted back
at me. Looking down from our balcony below on the terrace there was
a large marble courtyard and I thought Tom may have climbed and
fallen down to the courtyard below. I then decided that I embarrassingly
needed to start looking for him in bedrooms. Eventually, I found him
sound asleep in a big wing chair in the bedroom of fellow guests Ben and
Doris Driver. I crept into the room and was pushing Tom out of the door
when a voice from the bed said, 'Goodnight,' and I replied, 'Goodnight,'
as though it was a normal occurrence for me to be pushing my husband
out of someone's room in the middle of the night. The next day Tom had
no recollection of this at all. The Drivers later said they saw a white figure
but thought it was Bhaiya visiting his girlfriend, whose bedroom was
on the opposite side of the palace to his. They said, 'Goodnight, Bhaiya,'
whereupon the figure stopped and sank into the chair. They later awoke
and found me there pushing him out the door!

We were due to return to Calcutta the next morning aboard the main
Bengal express that went through Cooch Behar. We were to catch the
express at 9 am, but following Tom's sleepwalking episode, we remained
sound asleep in bed at that time. This was not a problem – for us, at least.
One of Bhaiya's aides knocked on our door saying, 'Madam, His Highness
said don't worry about the train. The train will be kept until you're ready.'
So we breakfasted late together before we all left for the train, which was
by that stage teeming with local people. It amazed me that the train had
been held for us; we even walked through a guard of honour to board it.

We alighted only half an hour later at Lamanihat, where American
servicemen in jeeps met us and took us to the airfield where we boarded a

China Transport plane for Calcutta – all this arranged by the US Air Force General staying at Cooch Behar for the shoot. I felt very guilty leaving the train to travel speedily and in such comfort on to Calcutta while those on the train continued in the heat and discomfort. Before leaving, Bhaiya gave Tom and me a beautifully bound book from the Cooch Behar library. It was his grandfather's shooting log of fifty years of shooting in Cooch Behar. He insisted that we return and stay during the good shooting season. It had been a perfect few days and an incredible introduction to India and my new life there in which I would become a part of the last days of the British Raj.

Lady Rutherford arrived on Thursday 12 October to take me to Bihar, though it was a couple of days before we left Calcutta, so there were more frivolities. There was a cocktail party in the house for about sixty mainly service people, which included a few Australians. Afterwards Tom and I, with Lady Rutherford, Sir John Birda, Air Commodore Francis Mellersh and David Clowes, also a British Army ADC to Mr Casey, dined at Firpos restaurant with Tony Sanger and his wife, Ira. Tony Sanger was one of the world's best polo players. Francis Mellersh – known as 'Tog' – was Air Commander for the Strategic Air Force Eastern Air Command and was a jolly soul who always hosted fabulous parties. We had a grand night and carried on at Club 300 after. While still in Calcutta, we also squeezed in another visit to Tolly Gunge to attend the races. On my last night, we went around to Club 300 after dinner to bid farewell to everyone. There I met film star Melvyn Douglas, who was in India to entertain American troops. He was exactly the same as on screen. Melvyn Douglas later told Tom he had been 'very taken with me', which I thought was very flattering. In today's terms it would be like having George Clooney say he was taken with me!

My first two weeks in Calcutta had been spent largely in a round of parties, although the war remained close by, with uniformed people in the crowds and the fighting in Burma so near. Life was to become more settled when I went to Bihar to take up my position as lady-in-waiting.

CHAPTER 5

Being part of the British Raj

Lady Rutherford and I left Calcutta by plane on Sunday morning 15 October 1944 bound for Ranchi, the summer capital of Bihar. I was full of excitement and looking forward to seeing what was to be my new home. The provincial capital, Government House and central administration were in Patna. Bihar was primarily an agricultural province immediately east of Bengal. Ranchi was 652 metres above sea level and the weather there was quite different to that in Calcutta – we did not need to use fans at all. Ranchi itself was like a pleasant country town, with Government House similar to a large country home in England. The surrounding countryside was most picturesque and the gardens of Government House were spectacular with eighty *mahli* (gardeners)

Government House, Ranchi.

employed to maintain them. Growth was incredibly rapid and the sweeping lawns of Government House were completely taken up and replaced in one season. On some hot summer nights the servants would erect a makeshift bedroom entirely of mosquito nets on the lawns and I would sleep there, waking up amid the beautiful flowerbeds. This came to an end when I complained to the housekeeper that I thought the servants must have been eating too much garlic as there was a very strong and

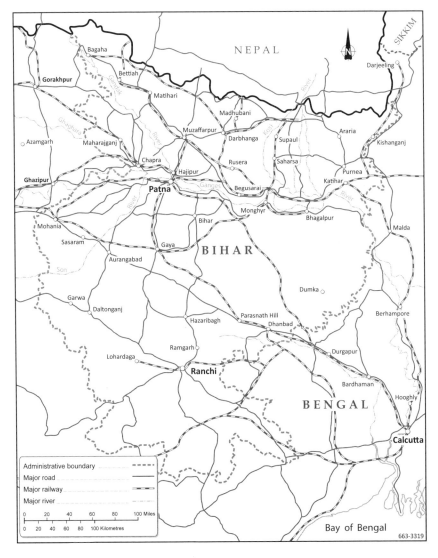

MAP 4: Bihar State, India (Michael Ross).

unpleasant smell of garlic in the area. I discovered, however, that one of the most beautiful trees in the garden was shedding seeds and the smell was coming from this, the tree being known as a garlic tree. In the future we kept clear of that area until the seeds in the pods were all shed.

The Rutherfords were warm and charming and treated me like a family member. I had my own sitting room, furnished in a gold-coloured brocade, a bedroom done in chintz and a lovely bathroom. I also had the use of a car and driver whenever I needed. The household consisted of Viscount Lord Pollington, Sir Thomas Rutherford's ADC, the Honourable Francis Balfour, son of Lord Riversdale who was military secretary, a household of servants, and Mrs Carpenter, the housekeeper. Soon afterwards Robin Cameron, whom I had known growing up in Perth and who had enlisted in the RAAF, joined Sir Thomas's staff as his ADC. Robin contacted me when he had finished an operational tour and was due for a new appointment, and asked me about a vacant ADC position. I introduced him to Sir Thomas Rutherford who promptly invited him to join a bird shoot later that day. Robin evidently made a good impression because he joined the staff before Christmas. There was also a houseguest when I arrived, the Under-Secretary of State to India, Lord Munster. He was a pleasant, short, and jolly man who was visiting Ranchi on welfare work.

Mrs Carpenter was a most important person in the household, being the housekeeper for the government houses at Ranchi and Patna, and she and her kitchen staff would move whenever the Rutherfords changed houses. Mrs Carpenter was a small, thin Englishwoman with grey hair and dry withered skin after years of being in India's climate. She routinely wore a long, high round-necked dress made of dullish grey material with a wide belt of the same. Being a very private person I do not believe any of us knew her story or if she had family in India, and she always wore a frown. But first-class food always came out of her kitchen and some of my favourite recipes of hers I made for my guests after I returned to Australia.

I was not being paid as Lady Rutherford's lady-in-waiting, but I had my own personal servant provided – Mahabir – who went everywhere with me. The system of servants was as formalised as any Australian trade union and all servants had their strict duties. If I wanted a cup of tea, I would say to Mahabir, 'Would you please get me a cup of tea?' He would then go to the door and ask the same thing of the *chaparasi* there,

Chicken Firpo Gov House, Bihar, India

Chicken, flour, 2 oz cream, 2 oz butter, 2 tomatoes, salt and pepper

METHOD. *Melt butter in pan – cut part cooked chicken into small sections. Cover well with flour, salt and pepper, and cook for 10 minutes. Add cream and chopped tomato, and cook 5–7 mins. Serve straight from fire.*

Chicken American Gov House, Bihar, India

Chicken, breadcrumbs, egg, paprika, butter, vegetable stock, flour, 2 cups cream

METHOD. *Cut chicken into pieces as for sauté. Pepper and salt. Roll each piece in egg and breadcrumbs, and cook in a good quantity of sizzling butter basting from time to time. When chicken thoroughly cooked, remove from pan and keep warm. If the sauce left in the pan is too fatty it may be skimmed. In the same pan, put a little flour and the vegetable stock and stir until smooth. Then add cream and paprika to taste. Make sure the sauce does not boil or curdle. To serve, pour sauce over chicken.*

Byculla Souffle

¹/₂ pt cream, 1 oz gelatin, 1 liqueur glass sherry, rum or brandy, 2 oz sugar, 3 eggs, crushed Ratofias [sweet biscuits]

METHOD. *Beat cream & sugar till smooth. Dissolve gelatin in little water & add. Beat yolks & white separately until of fair consistency, then combine. Together add to whipped cream mixture. Add sherry or rum. Pour into a soufflé dish lined with crusted Ratofias & before serving sprinkle crushed Ratofias on top.*

Favourite recipes brought back from Government House, India.

who would go to the next door with the same request. There might be six servants involved before the request reached the kitchen, and the tray of tea would then be relayed back to me in the same order. At first I found it frustrating, but it was simply something one had to accept, and it created jobs for a great number of people.

I quickly settled into my routine of lady-in-waiting. Every morning, on my dressing table, I would find a small booklet telling me the engagements and my program for the day – which car I would be travelling in, the order in which the cars would be driven, and which servants would accompany us. It was unlike anything I had ever experienced. I was responsible for arranging Lady Rutherford's official engagements, attending to her correspondence in conjunction with and making all her official engagements, and writing thank-you notes.

My work also entailed visiting wounded troops in hospital. Ranchi was the biggest hospital area for the wounded brought from Burma during the war, and Lady Rutherford and I would visit the hospitals several times a week and talk to the men, making sure they received their Red Cross parcels. I also helped out at the canteen, serving soldiers milk shakes and other items including cigarettes. The canteens were run by the Women's Voluntary Service (WVS), which had been established in England in 1938 as part of the Civil Defence Organisation. Stella Isaacs, the Dowager Marchioness of Reading, established branches of the WVS in India during the war. She was the founder and chairman of the WVS in England and its champion during World War II. She was in India to oversee the work being undertaken by its 10,000 members. A capable and totally fearless woman, she invited Tom and me to stay when we visited England. She was later awarded five honorary doctorates, created Baroness Swansborough, and was the first woman peer to take a seat in the House of Lords.

The Americans also had camps in and around Ranchi. For the American camps, interior designers had used glamorous décor and furnishings, including inexpensive but effective indirect lighting, though to my eyes it looked as though no expense had been spared! They also had their own radio programs and received speeches for the presidential campaign as they happened. Most importantly, they had what to we girls was the ultimate luxury – silk stockings! One night I dined at one of the nearby American camps and ate hamburgers before watching the latest film from the United States.

My duties with the Rutherfords also required me to attend meetings of the Red Cross and WVS, and to visit town hospitals, schools and children's health centres. Visits to the children's health centres were an important part of the duties of the governor's wife, and the wellbeing of these centres became something of a crusade for Lady Rutherford. Previous governor's wives had persuaded the government to establish a new child health centre, which they had duly done and named it after her, but funding for each would run out after the governor's wife moved on and a new centre would be made for the next governor's wife. Lady Rutherford sought to persuade the government of the time to provide for the existing centres as opposed to creating a new one in her name, which she did to great effect. This was particularly significant as at this time India was suffering a disastrous famine. Poor emaciated mothers with their starving babies would come in their droves to the centres and line up to get their thin claw-like hands on tins of lactogen. They were then lined up along the boundary where they could be seen feeding their babies. The tragedy of this was that if these mothers were not made to give their babies the food there, their own starvation might tempt them to sell it on the black market.

My work also involved lengthy tours with Lady Rutherford when she accompanied her husband, Sir Thomas, who was required to make regular visits to different parts of the province to visit the British Residents in each district and to ensure the states were being run properly. It was like a regular audit. Each tour was organised by Government House staff, and observed all the appropriate protocols so as not to disappoint the prominent people who invited the governor and his party to stay with them.

During these tours, while Sir Thomas attended to the business of administering the province, Lady Rutherford and I would visit prominent women of the district, as well as hospitals and schools, where there would often be festivities in our honour. Girls and boys were educated separately. It was usual for upper-class Indians to educate their sons in England, while daughters were either educated at home or sent to a local school. Many girls' schools were *purdah* schools, which allowed them to grow up in accordance with those values.

The word *purdah* literally means curtain, and describes the practice where Hindu and Muslim women remain separate from men, showing their faces to male family members only. The practice had originally been identified with Muslim women, but over centuries of Muslim rule in India, had been adopted by Hindu women. The practice was no longer universal among Hindu women but there were many older, conservative women who still practised strict *purdah*.

We were always very diplomatic during these tours, ensuring we visited any maharanis (the maharaja's wives), important Indian women, and women in *purdah*. We made a point of meeting these women in *purdah* and accepting all their invitations. These visits, or *purdah* parties as we called them, gave the women great pleasure. They were curious to get a glimpse of us and learn about our lives since we were so foreign to their world, and they went to great trouble to prepare for our visits. However, these could also be rather trying and stilted affairs due to the vast cultural divide, the status accorded the governor's wife, and because Lady Rutherford and I could speak almost no Hindi and most of the *purdah* women couldn't speak English. During one particular party I had to insist Lady Rutherford visit the rest room as the women had gone to a lot of trouble to create a special 'retiring room' with a Western toilet for her visit. After she had addressed all the women, they kept asking her if she wished to retire, to which she kept replying, 'No, thank you.' I finally whispered to her, 'You just *must* retire.' There was great excitement as she stood to 'retire': they all rose to their feet and were delighted that she would use the special toilet they had prepared for her.

There were always large crowds to see the governor drive through the villages and often big welcome signs erected at the entrance and exit. One which amused us, was a large sign saying 'WELL-COME' as we entered, and as we left there was a large sign saying 'WELL-GONE'. We trusted it was only wishing us a good journey!

One of my first official tours with Lady Rutherford occurred towards the end of October, soon after I had arrived. We left Ranchi early in the morning and drove to Hazaribagh, where Lady Rutherford and I inspected several reform schools, ordinary schools and missions. We then continued on to Padma and the palace of Maharajah Bahadur Kamakshya Narain Singh, of Ramgarh. It was enormous with a long

A typical reception for Lady Rutherford, 1944.

drive leading up to it. We were met and directed to the guesthouse – as only close relations and intimate acquaintances were permitted to stay in the palace. On our arrival, the Rajah's small son stepped forward and placed a type of lei made of spun gold around both of our necks.

The guesthouse was pleasant but I had to use a real Indian bathroom for the first time. The toilet consisted of an enamel jerry on a stand and a bath. My servant had to bring the water whenever I had a bath and I had to squeeze into the tiny tub and endeavour to scrub myself. So far I had found the toilet facilities in the palaces and homes of those I had visited to be modern and similar to what I was accustomed, so this was an entirely new experience. I wrote of our stay there:

> Everything everywhere reeking of wealth. Dining room table lacquered in this floral pattern and covered with glass. Each wall hung with enormous painting of Indian dancing woman. Ate soup (pea!) Roast beef and vegetable Curry (either prawn or egg) and steamed pears. Went on down after to see two live tigresses in pit. Terrific looking animals – one nearly got Minnie [Lady Rutherford's dog] as she ran past the bars of the cage.
>
> [Diary, 27.10.1944]

We paid a visit to the Rani, the elderly mother and Rajkumari of Kurda, who was Nepalese and still a very attractive woman. She had with her an equally beautiful young cousin, Raya, aged about thirty. Both of them were in *purdah*, yet they wanted to be active in the world and not simply observers, so we talked with the Rajah about what we believed to be the inequity of keeping women separate.

On our first night the women brought out their jewellery at Lady Rutherford's request, and what a time we had! They had every kind of gem imaginable, and all of them beautifully set. Every necklace had matching rings, two matching bracelets, two amulets, two brooches and earrings. It took us three hours to look at everything. We were told, however, that the superior pieces were in the museum. On our last night, Rani and Raya had a wonderful time dressing me for dinner in one of their gorgeous saris and covering me in jewels. The sari was gorgeous – all pastel tinted tissue interwoven with real silver thread.

As guests of the Rajah of Ramgarh, we went shooting in the jungle during the day. Instead of shooting from elephants we did so from mounted *machans*, safety platforms set in trees. The 1000 or so beaters formed a semi-circle about two kilometres away and herded the tigers and other animals towards us.

A typical picnic lunch while on tour, 1944.

Government House, Patna, 1944.

After Padma we motored on to Patna, stopping for a picnic lunch on our way. Patna was the capital and commercial centre of Bihar on the banks of the Ganges. It was a sacred city for the Sikhs and one of the oldest continuously inhabited places in the world and an ancient seat of learning and fine arts. Patna was full of interesting people, among them Diwan Bahadur Radkrishna Jalan, one of the world's most renowned jade collectors. He invited Lady Rutherford to view his famed collection and I accompanied her to his large home, *Jalan House*. We had a colourful reception from members of his household who placed golden garlands around our necks. We then proceeded to go from room to room seeing his amazing collection. Each room was devoted to a different colour: *Famille Blanche*, *Famille Rose* and *Famille Verte*. Glass shelves went from ceiling to floor displaying these beautiful works of art and the Rai Bahadur explained to us the importance of the most rare, though all were objects of great beauty and wonder. Many of the private treasures of India were lost to the world in later years. *Jalan House* is now a museum, and its works of art remain for the public to enjoy.

Patna was enjoyable after Calcutta and Ranchi, though it seemed to me that there were no young people about at all. The city was also much hotter than Ranchi, which meant that we had dinner at about 9 pm by candlelight on the terrace off the dining room. It was very romantic

3

TRANSPORT ORDER.

PATNA.

NOVEMBER 1944—
Tuesday, 7th.

6-15 A.M. Lady Rutherford's & Mrs. Porter's bearers with luggage of the Party and Tilloo with arrangements for **Breakfast** and **Picnic lunch** will leave for Patna Jn. in **C. H. car No. 4**

MIRZAPUR.

Transport at Mirzapur to and from Collector's house will be arranged by the servants themselves

BUXAR.

Wednesday, 8th.

5-30 A.M. Immediately on arrival of the train at **Buxar** Tilloo will go to the Refreshment Room where the Manager will give him arrangements for **early tea.** Tilloo will carry a basket and Thermos flask for this purpose

DINAPORE.

8-55 A.M. The servants will return to Government House in **C. H. car No. 4**

F. H. BALFOUR, MAJOR,
Military Secretary to His Excellency
the Governor of Bihar.

B.G.H.P. (M.S.G.) No. C471—15—4-11-1944.

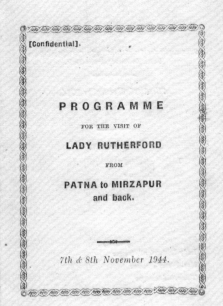

[Confidential].

PROGRAMME

FOR THE VISIT OF

LADY RUTHERFORD

FROM

PATNA to MIRZAPUR
and back.

7th & 8th November 1944.

Programme for the visit of Lady Rutherford from Patna to Mirzapur and back.

7th & 8th November 1944,

THE PARTY.

Lady Rutherford
Mrs. R. E. Porter

Servants.
Lady Rutherford's bearer
Mrs. Porter's bearer
Tilloo, khidmatgar

2

PROGRAMME.

NOVEMBER 1944—
Tuesday, 7th.

6-25 A.M. Lady Rutherford accompanied by Mrs. Porter will leave for Patna Jn. in **C. H. car No. 1**
6-30 A.M. Arr. Patna Jn.
　　　　　 Entrain*
6-38 A.M. Dep. Patna Jn.—By 5-Up
　　　　　 Breakfast on train
10-34 A.M. Arr. Moghalsarai
11-07 A.M. Dep. do. —By 7-Up
12 NOON **Picnic lunch** on train
12-25 P.M. Arr. Mirzapur
　　　　　 Detrain
　　　　　 Met by Mr. K. S. Misra, Collector of Mirzapur and Mrs. Misra
　　　　　 Proceed to Collector's house
　　　　　 (Car arranged by the Collector)
　　　　　 Visit Messrs. Obeetee Ltd. and Messrs. E. Hill & Co.
　　　　　 Tea
8-30 P.M. **Dinner**
9-30 P.M. Dep. Collector's house
　　　　　 Arr. Mirzapur Ry. Station
9-45 P.M. Entrain*
10-51 P.M. Dep. Mirzapur—By 2-Down
Wednesday, 8th.
00-02 A.M. Arr. Moghalsarai
03-10 A.M. Dep. do. —By 26-Down
　　　　　 Early tea
8-55 A.M. Arr Dinapore
　　　　　 Detrain and proceed to Government House in car No. 1
　　　　　 Breakfast

* A coupe has been reserved on an extra through coach.

Official programme for tour from Patna to Mirzapur, November 1944.

eating beneath the moon and stars. Government House was close to the centre of the city. It was a large two-storey house with a glorious garden and a new swimming pool. The house itself, though, was not well looked after, and one of my tasks while in Patna was to redecorate the house. Lady Rutherford left it to me as she thought it was such a hopeless job. I was happy to take on the challenge and decided to start with my room. I wanted all my furniture painted cream and the walls a faint pastel green. I decorated the sitting room adjoining my bedroom with the same colour scheme. I redecorated the walls and set about getting chintzes and material for the curtains, chairs and bedspreads. I had the chairs and sofa covered in a rather nice course cream cotton material, and had green and cream striped cushions made. Once my rooms were finished, I started on the others. I enjoyed the challenge, and eventually every room had been decorated in a different pastel toning with coordinated furniture. It all looked charming and Lady Rutherford was thrilled.

Our decorating demands meant we had to travel to Mersapur – the most famous carpet-making town in India – where the carpets were made by hand and never wore out. We left Government House in Patna early in the morning, arriving at the railway station under police escort. We

The official party before the Governor's train, 1944.
Lady Rutherford second from left, me third from right.

boarded the governor's special coach, which had been added to the train and which was carpeted throughout and consisted of a suite of rooms. We travelled with three servants who prepared our bunks at night, unpacked and repacked our cases, and prepared our meals. There was a police guard outside the carriage at every station and all sorts of fuss and bother everywhere. We arrived in the early afternoon at Mersapur, which was an old town and architecturally fascinating. The huts were made of old bricks about fifteen centimetres long by seven centimetres wide, and the streets were frightfully narrow, with funny little buildings with low doors, and some old buildings tilted at about thirty degrees! It was quite an incredible sight.

ABOVE: On tour in Bihar, 1944. *Left to right from centre:* Lady Rutherford, John Pollington, me, Robin Cameron.

RIGHT: Gurkha Guard with bagpipes, Government House, Ranchi, 1944.

The District Commissioner and his wife, both Indian, met us at the railway station and took us to the carpet-making places. We chose about sixteen carpets, all in plain colours, and also ordered one to be made for the staircase at Ranchi. We continued until late afternoon. Before we left, we visited the Commissioner's house, where we took tea and had a rest. We dined in the evening before returning home on the train. By then our carriage had been hitched to another train returning to Patna that night. We had the carpets put on to the train, as well as four live turkeys and goodness knows whatever else, all of which we had been given to us.

There was less of a social whirl in Bihar, but the government houses at both Patna and Ranchi were still the centres of the social scene. On Mondays and Fridays when not touring, I went to the old Government House – now called *Audrey House* after Lady Rutherford who had inspired its restoration for entertaining the troops. On Mondays an American band would pay for their troops and I regularly went and danced with them. One night, the Duke of Aostas' band, which had been brought out from America, played for us.

We also entertained many visitors at government house, though not on the Casey's lavish scale. Francis Balfour was away with Sir Thomas on one occasion, which left John Pollington and me, together with Lady Rutherford, holding the fort. Three American service personnel came for the weekend and we played plenty of tennis and had an enjoyable time. They had come laden with gifts, presenting me with a box of Whitmans chocolates, nail polish and remover, and cosmetics. An American, General Cheeves, from Calcutta, also sent me a two-gallon thermos flask with a small tap so I had iced water 'on tap' in my room all day, which was quite a luxury in wartime.

CHAPTER 6

Touring Again

Sir Thomas, Lady Rutherford and I went on another extensive tour of Bihar in early December. On this occasion, we sailed up the Ganges on a paddle steamer for a mile or so and then boarded a train, where I had a whole coach to myself, including a bathroom. We arrived at Begusarai and spent the afternoon touring the village hospitals. Another requirement of touring was for Sir Thomas and Lady Rutherford to lay foundation stones. This was a rather interesting custom of putting silver money and the newspaper of the day in a jar, inserting it in a space in a wall and laying a stone on top of it, so that in centuries to come it will be a record for historians or archaeologists. Everywhere we went Sir Thomas and Lady Rutherford were treated like royalty. They were seated on real gold and silver thrones from where they delivered speeches.

A welcome while on tour, 1944.

Sir Thomas Rutherford said of the cheering crowds when we arrived at Begusarai, 'You never know whether the crowds were screaming *laht Sahib ki jai* (welcome) or *laht Sahib ki jao* (go).' Ghandi was promoting Indian independence, so riots were not uncommon. Lady Rutherford and I also understood this confusion. On a visit to a school, one little girl gave an impassioned speech and kept pointing at us in a manner that we found quite alarming as we did not understand what was being said. We later found out that she was praising us in the most flowery language.

The day at Begusarai was a great success. The train departed early the next morning while most of us were still sleeping and arrived in Purnea, about 140 kilometres away, around late morning. Again we did the usual tour of hospitals and schools and attended a public meeting at the Town Hall. That afternoon Lady Rutherford and I also went off to a *purdah* party where, fortunately for us, most of the women spoke English. Afterwards, we attended a garden party where I sat next to Maharajah P.C. Lall who hosted a dinner for us that evening.

> The grounds were a mass of lights as we approached and as we entered the drawing room were met by a blaze of Venetian glass, Chandeliers, silver and gold sarees, jewels (and rather dowdy brown and gold brocade furniture!). [Diary, 6.12.1944]

Tours were not just devoted to official business, and Maharajah P.C. Lall took us duck shooting about eighteen miles from Purnea. We drove at first and then went on elephants until we came to a place called Jihl, where there were dozens of ducks. I managed to shoot a duck, much to my joy. Afterwards we had a most marvellous seven-course lunch, and *shamianas* had been erected as well as dressing rooms and bathrooms.

Lunch after the duck shoot, Simri Bakhtiarpur, North Bihar, December 1944.

Early the next day we left and headed for Kishangarh, about sixty-five kilometres away on the dustiest of roads. Once again, Lady Rutherford and I attended a *purdah* party, which turned out to be something of an ordeal. We sat at a table covered in beautiful gold brocade with gold and silver chairs while the Indian women sat around and stared at us. These women were in strict *purdah* and this was their treat. We tried to engage them in conversation but none of the local women spoke English.

The next day was another early start, this time heading for Katihar. Lady Rutherford and I visited the WVS workers, all of whom were Anglo-Indians. Unfortunately, the refreshments served to us consisted of dreadful coffee and awful cakes, which we duly ate out of politeness. We

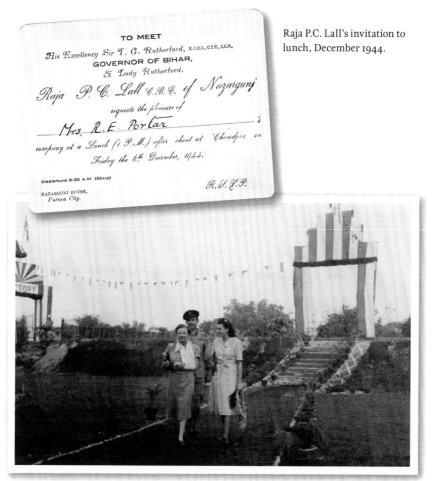

Raja P.C. Lall's invitation to lunch, December 1944.

With Lady Rutherford at Kishangarh, December 1944.

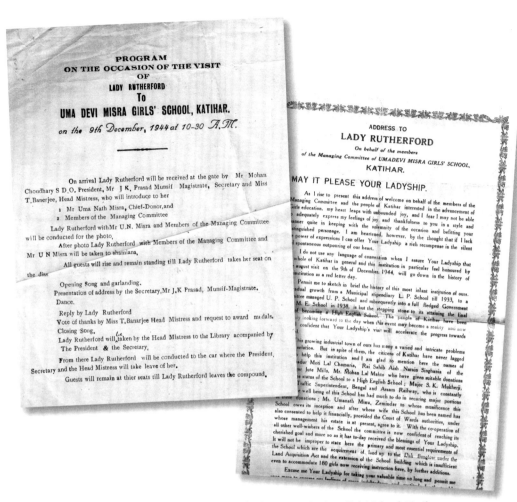

Program and address to Lady Rutherford, Uma Devi Misra Girls' School, Katihar, December 1944.

then went to an Indian girls' school, where three small girls danced in the loveliest costumes imaginable with garlands of flowers woven their hair and around their necks.

Another wondrous experience occurred on this tour. Nawab Chandri hosted dinner for us at Simri Bakhtiapur in his guesthouse, which was not particularly spectacular, but where we dined off solid silver plates and had French champagne for the first time in ages. Even John – Viscount Lord Pollington, who later became the Earl of Mexborough, and who was a teetotaller – was tempted by it.

We had another wonderful experience after Simri Bakhtiapur. We left the train early in the morning and drove to a tributary of the Kosi River through tiny villages. After crossing rivers and riding elephants, we came to a stretch of water massed with ducks. The group shot quite a few, after which we enjoyed a picnic lunch provided by the Nawab of Bahktiarpur.

On our way to a school at Simri Bakhtiapur, December 1944.

On our way to Saharsa, December 1944.

The picnic was set out on a beautiful brocade ground sheet and servants waited on us. The dinner service was fine china and silver cutlery that had been sent ahead by the Nawab with the servants. Later, we had tea at the Nawab's palace and met his wife and daughter, both of whom were beautiful and wearing lavish jewels.

Our tour then continued aboard a ferry down the Ganges from Monlighat to Monghyr, passing picturesque scenes of old sailing boats. At Monghyr, Lady Rutherford and I attended yet another *purdah* party – this time at the home of Mrs Deranasir Prasad Singh. We were met first by the men who wore turbans adorned with rich jewels, who ushered us upstairs where all the walls were tiled with bright colours and unusual designs. Even the shades on the lights were made of coloured glass with intricate patterns. The *purdah* party room was also tiled: with the women in brightly coloured saris and smothered in jewels it reminded me of something out of a film.

ABOVE: Crossing a river while on tour, 1944. TOP: A picnic while on tour, 1944.

LEFT: Aboard the governor's train while on tour, 1944, with Enid de Salis (second from right).

A welcome party on tour, Bihar, 1944.

Visiting local children affected by the drought, 1944.
Left to right: Lady Rutherford, 'Plum' Rutherford.

After leaving Monghyr we visited a girls' school at Khagariato, where they put on a gymnastic demonstration for Lady Rutherford. It was rather quaint. All the girls dressed in bright yellow saris and performed ancient Mogul dances with swords and knives. That evening we dined at the home of Baboo Lalatishwar Prasad Singh at Salaman. The next day we went on yet another duck shoot and later lunched in style in a magnificent tent and ate goose kabala, a delicious Indian dish. We saw thousands of ducks and geese on the second stretch of water.

Next was Rusera, then Bukanti and finally Kashiwayri, where we distributed blankets and saris to about 1500 destitute people. The drought had affected people all over India and many were in need. After, we lunched as guests of the Maharajah of Darbhanga in the Government Circuit House at Bedorli before returning to the train to proceed to Hajipur, where Lady Rutherford distributed prizes at the girls' school.

I saw much of Bihar during the course of our tours, and saw a very different way of life. I saw peasant women pounding rice to separate the husks, the way they cooked and what they ate, which to me appeared terribly primitive. Happily, during my time in India, I never lacked for generous amounts of food prepared by chefs in hygienic kitchens, although I remained careful about salads. And not surprisingly, we ate a great deal of curry. Sir Thomas Rutherford loved curries and a curry dish was obligatory on Sundays. He insisted that a curry could not be considered good unless it was so hot that the perspiration ran down one's face!

Calcutta visits

I managed to visit Tom in Calcutta in between tours with Sir Thomas and Lady Rutherford and during breaks in his busy schedule. In November 1944, the household of Calcutta Government House had gone to the summer station at Darjeeling. At the same time there was a governors' wives conference in Delhi from 22 to 24 November. Instead of going with Lady Rutherford to the conference, she agreed that I could visit Tom in Calcutta. Tom and I managed rather well looking after guests and generally holding the fort. It was quite a surprise to find myself as the hostess of this grand palace. In fact, we thought we managed everything with greater success than when the entire household was there, all the guests certainly seemed to enjoy themselves.

These brief visits were rather hectic. Tom and I would go riding early every morning. Then one night we had Lawrence Pratt and a woman called Ann Lycett to dine, and later joined Tog Mellersh and Ira Sanger, wife of Tony, at Club 300. We did not return home till early the next day but rose at the usual time and rode for an hour before going to the race-track for the early morning gallops, as we did each day, and later played tennis for hours without a break. I was certainly weary afterwards. That night we had the Countess of Carlisle to dine, as well as a Miss Collins and a couple of others, and so I played hostess once more. Another day we lunched at the swimming club where we sat around the pool at tables under umbrellas – I was with Doris Driver, one of the few people of my age I had been able to truly befriend. Other activities included a lunch with Tog Mellersh at Belvedere, which had been the Viceroy's Calcutta house and was now turned over to others, and a party given by Sir Renwick Haddow at his house where a dance floor had been put down on the lawn in his floodlit garden.

A fascinating guest whom I met at a luncheon party at Government House was Colonel Grant Taylor, who was employed by Britain's Scotland Yard. The British government had arranged for him to be lent to the American Federal Bureau of Investigation (FBI) during the 1920s and he was instrumental in the roundup of the great gangsters Al Capone and John Dillinger. With the outbreak of war, he became involved with combined operations, teaching commandoes the use of small arms. In 1941 he led a six-man team to Norway to kill eleven enemy collabora-tors and then to kill a group of Luftwaffe officers in France. He operated in Italy, the Middle East and the Far East under Field Marshal Slim's 14th Army in Burma. When I met him, he was at Fort Belvedere in Calcutta teaching the GIs to shoot. He invited me to join his shooting class, joining the GIs who had then advanced to learning to shoot with their left hand. When my turn came I was given a Colt automatic. Looking down to the end of the shooting gallery, I did exactly what the Colonel told me, and my three shots resulted in three bullseyes! His instructions, among others, were to have my elbow in line with my belly button, to look at my target and to squeeze the trigger like an orange. I had started the war by practising giving injections into oranges and was now learning to shoot to kill by squeezing an orange. I must say that Tom, who had accompanied me with the expectation of having a good laugh, treated me with great respect on the trip home.

Indian summer

Each year as the weather became warmer, the entire household would move to the summer station Government House in the hills north of Ranchi. This was a mind-boggling operation as the moving instructions (over page) indicate. I find the careful instructions for the 'Radiogramophone' evidence not only of the momentous occasion this was but also of how far radio communication had come. I also was amazed to be able to rise as normal in Patna, breakfast, board the train, arrive at Ranchi and be able to bathe and change into clean clothes already hanging in my cupboard!

My routine of touring and socialising eventually gave way to the celebration of Christmas and the New Year, both of which were unforgettable. Christmas Day 1944 proved to be another incredible experience in this remarkable land. We left Patna two days before Christmas and journeyed

The camp provided for one of the tiger shoots, Christmas 1944.

Move of His Excellency's Household, etc., from Government House, Patna, to Government House, Ranchi, in April 1945.

APRIL 1945—
Sunday, 8th.

Heavy baggage containing household and personal effects, teutage, office records, press materials, Darbar paraphernalia, etc., will be loaded on six wagons at the P.W.D. siding on the 8th, 9th and 10th April. These wagons will be loaded and made over to the railway by 1-00 P.M. on the 10th April and despatched to Ranchi. Transhipment at Muri will be carried out by the Sub-Inspector of Police who will send intimation of their arrival at Ranchi to Messrs. Rattanlal Surajmal, who will supply the necessary transport.

The Sub-Inspector of Police & Sonalal Singh, with two constables and one tent khalasi will proceed to Muri *via* Barkakana by the train leaving Patna at 17-38 hours on the 10th April to supervise transhipment of goods at Muri on the 12th.

20 bullock carts ... ⎫ From 7-00 A.M. to 5-00 P.M. on 8th &
⎬ 9th and up to 12 NOON on the 10th at
Government House lorry ⎭ Government House, Patna.

Wednesday, 11th.

The servants noted in the margin* will go to Ranchi in advance by train according to the following timings :—

17-25 Dep. Patna Junction.

*One cook.
One khidmatgar,
One under bearer.
One maaalchi.
Arjun, tub boy.
Two dhobies
Two sweepers.
Two chaprasis.
One office khalasi.
One constable.

Thursday, 12th.
8-09 Arr. **Ranchi Road.**

Govt. House bus ⎫ At Govt. House, Patna on
Govt. House lorry ⎬ 11th at 3-00 P.M.
10 coolies ... ⎭

One 30-seater ⎫ At Ranchi Road Railway
lorry. ⎬ Station on the 12th at
10 coolies ... ⎭ 8-00 A.M.
10 coolies at Govt. House, Ranchi.

Thursday, 12th.

(1) 3-00 P.M. Five horses under supervision of Capt. Abdul Latif Khan will be loaded in a Horse-box at Patna Jn. which will be attached to the special train. At Muri they will be transhipped to Narrow-gauge special.

(2) 4-30 P.M. All servants with families (excepting those mentioned above and in the tour booklets) will travel to Ranchi in the special train according to the following timings :—

19-10 Dep. Hardinge Park.
6-20 Arr. Barkakana **on 13th.**
7-00 Dep. do.
8-30 Arr. Muri.
10-00 Dep. do.
12-30 Arr. Ranchi.

(3) Lt.-Col. R. A. de Salis, Captain and Mrs. R. E. Porter, Captain Abdul Latif Khan, Mrs. Carpenter and the following subordinate staff with their families will travel in the special train :—

Lt.-Col. R. A. de Salis ... ... One 1st class compartment.
Capt. & Mrs. R. E. Porter ... Do.
Captain Abdul Latif Khan ••• Do.
Mrs. Carpenter ... ... Do.
Mr. Owen's family ... ... One 2nd class compartment.
Mr. Potter's family ... ... Do.
H. K. Sanyal and family ... Do.
Dr S. D. Banerji and family ... Do.
A. H. Khan's family ... Do.
P. G. Sinha and family ... ... Do.
C. L. Kapoor's family ... Do.
A. C. Mukherji and family ... Do.
M. Zakaria and family ... ... Do.
Qamruzzaman Khan & family ... Do.

The Office Superintendent will leave on the morning of the 13th and arrive at Ranchi in the evening.

2

APRIL 1945—
Thursday, 12th.

(4) The families of drivers will travel in two small 3rd class compartments·

(5) The dhobies and sweepers will occupy one small third class compartment.

(6) Amiruddin's family will occupy one small third class compartment.

(7) The Special Guard constables with **Government cash** will occupy one side of a large compartment.

1-00 P.M. Radhika Singh, munshi and Siddique, Electrical mistry will securely pack the Government House **Radiogramophone** in its case and personally supervise its transport in the G.H. lorry from Government House to the special train at Hardinge Park. They will place it in a safe corner in the through brakevan. Thereafter Ismail, Transport munshi, will be responsible for its safety. He will also see that it is properly transhipped into the special at Muri and unloaded at Ranchi Railway Station and carried to Government House with special care. The Government House Overseer, Ranchi, will take charge of it as soon as it arrives at the House.

(Md. Ismail will take personal charge of His Excellency's **Radio set and Tour Radio set**).

The **Motor cycle** will also be loaded on this train and transhipped into the special at Muri.

Transport at Government House, Patna.

1-00 P.M. 10 bullock carts ⎫ At sub-staff quarters.
           8 coolies   ...⎭

3-00 P.M. Three bullock carts for fodder and saddlery.

4-00 P.M. Govt. House lorry.
           G. H. Bus.
           One passenger lorry.
           Six coolies.

5-00 P.M. 9 gharries for sub-staff.
           4 coolies.

6-00 P.M. One taxi for Captain Abdul Latif Khan.
           One taxi for Mrs. Carpenter.
           20 coolies at **Hardinge Park** from 4-00 P.M.

6-30 P.M. Lt.-Col. de Salis ⎫
           Mrs. Porter   ...⎬ G. H. car No. 1.
           Capt. R. E. Porter ⎭

At Muri.

Friday, 13th.

8-30 A.M. Lt.-Col. de Salis ⎫ Will leave for **Ranchi by road** in **G. H.**
           Mrs. Porter   ...⎬ **car No. 4** (which will be unloaded
           Capt. R. E. Porter ⎭ immediately after the arrival of the
                               special train).

           25 coolies. For transhipment of luggage from broad to narrow-gauge special.

At Ranchi Railway Station.

12 NOON   20 coolies.
          Four passenger lorries.
          Two open trucks.
          One taxi for Capt. Abdul Latif Khan.
          One taxi for Mrs. Carpenter.
          Ten bullock carts.

Movement of Government House cars.

Cars No. 1 & 2 and the Govt. House Bus will be used as per details in the Tour Booklets.

Car No. 3 will be sent to Ranchi Road by the train leaving Patna Junction at 6-57 hours on the 13th. Mohiuddin driver will load it on the van at Patna Jn. at 4-00 P.M. on the 12th. Badri Ram driver will drive the car from Ranchi Road to Ranchi on the morning of the **14th April.**

Govt. House lorry will be taken to Ranchi by road by Baiju Lall on the morning of the 13th April.

Car No. 4 will be taken on the special train on the 12th. It will be loaded at Patna Jn. at 4-00 P.M. by Badri Ram who will go in the special train.

R. A. de SALIS, Lt.-Col.,
Military Secretary to His Excellency
the Governor of Bihar.

about 115 kilometres along a canal road and into hills of dense jungle. We arrived at a place called Prattapur, in the Bihar jungle, in time for tea at the camp of Maharajah Kamakhya Narain Singh of Ramgarh, who had organised the occasion especially for Sir Thomas and Lady Rutherford. Others in our party included Francis Balfour, John Pollington, Robin Cameron, the ADCs, Mr E.O. Lee, John Halton, the Nawad of Bhaktapur, the Raja Basant Singh, his brother, Sri Palok Nake Singh, the Singhs of Buwari, and several Americans.

We had our camp, and the Maharajah of Ramgarh and his party had theirs. Our camp was quite grand and I wished my family could have seen it. We had a large carpeted tent furnished with a dressing table and a bathroom attached. We also had a large sitting room, with a blue carpet, pale green cane furniture and a fireplace in one corner, and this was attached to a dining room. We also had elephants and horses to ride on shoots when we could not take the cars. Words, however, cannot describe the Raja's camp, which was more luxurious than ours, even having the luxury of electric lighting. The *shamianas* were lined inside with rich brocades and the sitting room was enormous. The Maharajah's tent was heated with solid silver braziers and sunken pits of concrete where there were hot coals to warm the tent. They even put down a concrete dance floor.

Me on a country boat in Sombha Lake on way to the shoot, December 1944.

We camped at the foot of the Nepalese mountains, and with the mountains in the background and big fires throwing sparks into the air in the foreground, it was certainly a Christmas unlike any other.

On Christmas Eve we went on a tiger shoot after we had all settled in, although we didn't manage to shoot anything. That night there was a grand dinner party. We had cocktails in the sitting room and then walked over to the dining-room tent, where the tables were decorated with bright yellow cloths and sprinkled with silver 'snow'. There were also balloons, Christmas hats, crackers and streamers. Determined to have some form of Christmas tree I had even gone into the jungle and found a little tree and dressed it with decorations. Dinner consisted of tomato soup, turkey and ham, with plum pudding with brandy butter for dessert. As we walked out of dinner there was a huge bonfire and a fireworks display. We danced until late. After midnight I received my first Christmas present from Basant Singh, Raja's brother, it was a claw of the tiger shot at Ramgarh, which had been beautifully mounted on gold with an inscription on the back and made into a brooch. It was a wonderful memento of an unforgettable occasion, and proof of how right I had been to vow that I really believed in Father Christmas!

The tiger tooth brooch presented to me by Basant Singh at Christmas.

On Christmas morning we went on a shoot and returned with three lovely spotted deer but no tigers, despite hearing several around. There seemed to have been a difference of opinion among the beaters and so they messed up every beat we had, each time letting the tigers escape. It was still exciting sitting in the *machan* waiting for something to happen. That night we hosted the dinner party at our camp.

We had a most thrilling shoot before leaving the camp. A tiger had been reported in the area having made a kill. That day the group shot not one but three tigers. I saw all three, one of them a little too closely. This tiger came out of the jungle right in front of me while I was sitting in the *machan*, I became paralysed and could not shoot. I finally found my senses and, as I lifted my gun, I shouted at Sir Thomas who was in the *machan* with me, and he managed to shoot it. Sir Thomas said he looked at me,

On our way to a tiger shoot on this occasion sitting on Pads, 1944

The tiger shoot where a tiger and I 'made faces' at each other.

saw me rather white and staring ahead, and then looked and saw the
tiger making faces at me. This became one of his favourite party stories –
a tiger and me poking faces at one another.

My mother showed great concern with regard to my going shooting
and did not appear to have great confidence in me. As she wrote in a letter
to Tom: 'She seems to be having a wonderful time and a great experience,
but I hate the thought of her shooting. I know that you will think me
foolish but one hears of so many accidents and knowing June she is not
the most careful person I know!' [Letter, 15.02.45]

After the Christmas camp, I flew to Calcutta with Air Commodore
Francis Mellersh, who travelled regularly between Bihar and Bengal
and often found a place for me when going between Ranchi or Patna
and Calcutta. Happily I was able to celebrate New Year with Tom who
had been unable to obtain leave to join me on the Christmas camp. I
arrived in the early afternoon on New Year's Eve and accompanied the
Tom and the Caseys to the tennis championship finals as Tom was still on
duty with them. Later, at Government House, Ben and Doris Driver and
Tom's South African millionaire friend and shipping magnate, Leonard
Aldridge, called in to see us. Aldridge was another fascinating man. An
Englishman who had made his fortune conducting business based in
Egypt and extending through Africa and the Middle East, he had worked
with Mr Casey while the latter was Secretary of State based in Cairo. He
had been instrumental in using his business contacts to procure and
distribute wheat in Syria, Lebanon and Persia, helping to stave off social
unrest. He had offered his services to Casey to supply rice throughout
Bengal and to ease the conditions caused by the drought, which he did
without payment and much success.

Ed Greever and Gogo Berenson were also a part of the group that visited
us in Calcutta. Gogo, whose full name was Countess Maria Luisa Yvonne
Radha de Wendt de Kerlor, was the daughter of Elsa Schiaparelli, a famous
designer and a contemporary rival of Coco Chanel. Gogo was married to
a young American, Robert L. Berenson, nephew of the great art dealer
and collector Bernard Berenson. Robert had joined the American Navy,
and Gogo the American Red Cross, which sent her to India where I met
her. She had contracted malaria and was taken to hospital where Maie
Casey asked me to visit her. I had her brought to Government House to

Tom (*left*) and Ed Greever on the steps of Government House, Calcutta, 1944.

Gogo Berenson, Calcutta, 1944.

recuperate and we became great friends, and have remained so ever since.

Tom and I arranged to stay with Gogo as I did not want to stay at Government House and be tied down to all the formality. On New Year's Eve we dined with Sir Renwick Haddow and had a marvellous dinner party – though the other guests were not quite our vintage. We had been asked to several parties that night, and soon after midnight ten of our friends arrived *en masse* at the Haddows' to take us to other festivities. We first went to a club, and then to a party given by the Nawab of Marchidabad who had recently married a French woman. We returned to Gogo's flat about four hours after leaving the Haddows'. On New Year's morning we went to an 'eggnog party' organised by Syd de Kantzow, lunched at Club 300 with Leonard Aldridge, and then on to the races where I lost and Tom won 700 rupees. Tom surprised me with an emerald eternity ring, a ruby ring and some diamond and ruby earrings that were meant to be my Christmas present but did not arrive in time.

Before I returned to Patna, Gogo organised farewell drinks for me. I hated leaving Tom, but thankfully the Rutherfords were so kind to me. I wrote in one of my letters to my mother about the kind treatment of the Rutherfords, saying, 'They treat me just like a daughter. It couldn't be better.' We had a wonderful relationship and while Lady Rutherford had her foibles, I quickly learned how to accommodate these, and she and I worked extremely well together. Sir Thomas Rutherford was a brilliant man, very warm, and one of the finest men I have ever met.

CHAPTER 7

Vice-regal Life

Life had settled into something of a routine by early 1945. I continued to visit Tom in Calcutta whenever I could, and on one occasion the RAF gave me a lift in one of its Oxford planes, harnessed to a parachute and strapped to the seat, and arriving in just over an hour. I became a member of the Government House staff while I was there with Tom, and whenever anything special was happening in Calcutta I would be called on to come and stay at Government House and assist with entertaining the guests. There were also times when we were expecting important guests in Bihar, and Lady Rutherford would send me down to Calcutta to order anything special that was not available in Bihar.

Trips back and forth became unnecessary when Tom transferred to Bihar to succeed John Pollington as ADC to Sir Thomas in April 1945 and we were finally able to have lengthy periods together as husband and wife. Tom's move to Bihar also coincided with the end of the war in Europe and its impending end in Asia and the Pacific, making for an increasingly relaxed atmosphere.

Visiting Government House, Calcutta

At Government House in Calcutta, the Caseys entertained a great deal because of the many eminent guests and the military hierarchy that passed through. The dinner parties were grand affairs, with as many as fifty guests or more. On these occasions, it was important that the order of precedence be strictly adhered to so as not to give offence. The guests would gather in the Yellow Drawing Room before dinner and the ADCs would line them up in order of precedence for presentation to the governor. Tom and his colleagues would have spent a good part of the day studying who was to attend and learning their names and status so they had the order of precedence correct. Once lined up, Richard and Maie Casey would enter, walk down the line of guests and one or other of the ADCs would present each guest in turn to the Governor and his wife. They would then go in to dinner. The dining room very grand with large candelabra down the centre of the long table and a uniformed waiter behind each chair. After dinner, everybody would rise and drink to the King, after which the ladies withdrew to the Brown Drawing Room. After the men had their port and talk, they joined the ladies. The Caseys and guests would then engage in what we the staff called a game of 'Walkie-Talkie'. Richard Casey would be seated in one part of the room and Maie Casey in another. If someone had not had a chance to talk to either of them at dinner, an ADC would take them one by one. After about three minutes that person would be ushered away and another would be brought forward. I was fortunate to meet some extraordinary people at Calcutta Government House.

When Lady Rutherford left for Javeshedpur on 21 February 1945, it gave me the opportunity to fly down to Calcutta for a few days and do some shopping. Tom was not there to greet me but had sent a Government House car with a message to go straight to the races. We went out to dinner that night at Club 300 with a few friends and saw Lord Louis Mountbatten and his wife Edwina dining there. They stayed at Government House and so I saw a great deal of them. They were a most charming and colourful couple.

Lord Louis Mountbatten was born his Serene Highness Prince Louis of Battenberg and was an uncle of Prince Philip, Duke of Edinburgh. He commanded HMS *Kelly*, famous for many daring exploits during the Battle for Crete, but sunk in May 1941. Lord Louis was rescued with the other survivors. He had also been a very dashing social figure pre-war and married the great heiress the Honourable Edwina Ashley, the daughter of Wilfred Ashley, Baron Mount Temple, and Amalia Cassell. Edwina's grandfather, Sir Edward Cassell, had been a banker and financier and close friend of Edward VII.

A cocktail party was held the following evening in their honour. The guest list included General Linsdell, General Rooney, Brian Hunter, Captain David Clowes, the English ADC, Squadron Leader Dick Erskine Crum, Mountbatten's ADC, and Nancy Lees, Lady Louis's secretary, and Tom.

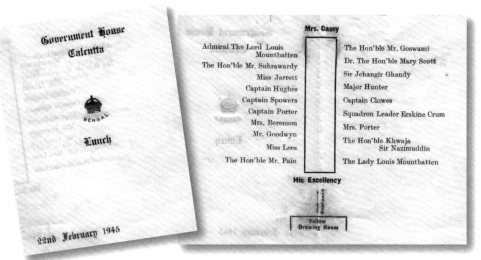

Lunch table plan, Government House, Calcutta, 22 February 1945.

Lord Louis Mountbatten was a very attractive and glamorous man and the competition between Gogo and me for his attention was fierce. I accused Gogo of having an unfair advantage over me with her Parisian dinner dresses. The ADCs who were responsible for the table seatings at each meal had great fun alternating Gogo and myself next to the 'Supremo' (Lord Louis). One luncheon party consisted of Tom, myself, Lord and Lady Mountbatten, Major Brian Hunter, Squadron Leader Dick Erskine Crum as well as a flock of generals and air marshals. I recorded that 'Gogo nearly swooned with delight' when she found she was seated next to the 'Supremo'. When I complained to Gogo that I thought he had talked far more to her at lunch than he had to me at dinner, she came back with, 'Good heavens! At dinner he was so engrossed with you his head was practically in your lap!' He was a delightful dinner companion and we talked on a variety of subjects, from the events that were unfolding around us to Australia, and he was most amused as to how I was able to get to India under the circumstances.

In the afternoons, Gogo and I would often swim or play tennis, and often Lord Louis came and sat with us for afternoon tea on the lawn. I always found it quite remarkable that this world renowned-figure would talk and laugh with us in such a relaxed manner.

The Mountbattens left next day much to the regret of Gogo and myself – we were now 'reduced to the two Captains again (Tom and Ed)'. [Diary, 24.2.1945] Lord Louis Mountbatten had been absolutely charming

Staff aboard aircraft, 1945.
Left side: Jane Casey, Richard Casey. *Right side:* Maie Casey, Tom, unknown.

and made everyone to whom he spoke feel important. I found Lady Louis to be a fascinating woman. She had an amazing mind and was a charming person. I did not think she was particularly good looking, but she had enormous personality. Tom's comment from a male perspective was that 'Lady Louis at forty-two looks her age and more, but is a rather striking woman'.

Some time later Lady Mountbatten came to visit Lady Rutherford and me to do the rounds of the various hospitals in Ranchi. We met her at the plane arriving from Calcutta and she said to me as she came down the steps, 'I've got a surprise for you.' Down behind her came the surprise – Tom! Knowing I was in Ranchi she had persuaded Richard Casey to let Tom have the day off to go to Ranchi with her so he could spend the day with me. Having him there certainly was a surprise, but even more so as the night before he had arrived home late and gone slap bang into one of the pillars in the 'Paris Underground', leaving his whole face covered in grazes. However, we had a marvellous day going around to the hospitals with Lady Mountbatten, and it was wonderful to see her capacity to lift the spirits of the wounded men.

Before Tom transferred to Bihar, I kept busy exploring India and its customs. During the course of our visit to Ramgarh and our shooting trip at Christmas, I had become friendly with the Maharajah's brother, his sister and his sister-in-law, and they discussed with me their desire to come out of *purdah*. I invited them to come and stay with us in Patna, and I became instrumental in introducing them to life outside *purdah*. They were very nervous eating their first meal around a dinner table in mixed company, so I told them to watch me and do everything that I did – I just hoped my table manners were not leading them astray! The Maharani was Nepalese, and was beautiful and softy spoken, as was 'Baby', the Maharajah's sister, whose ambition it was to drive a car.

Basant wrote me a lengthy letter afterwards:

On behalf of the ladies for your affectionate treatment and specially for the favour done to me by implanting into their minds the abominability of the purdah system, I am indeed very grateful to you. On return from the Govt. House I could notice some marked improvement in them. With a few more meetings and a little more effort I am positive that they will be able to shed their shyness forever. But this long interval in between makes me feel slightly apprehensive. It is not the building that makes the home, but it is the wife that makes it says a Sanskrit poet and how true it is! The roof that affords one shelter from heat and cold and rain is not to be judged by the pillars that support it – the finest Corinthian columns though they be – but by the real spirit pillar who is the centre, the real support of the home – the woman. Judged by that standard, the Indian home I regret to say hopelessly suffers in comparison with other homes in the world. There was a time when women in India used to occupy the foremost place in society but due to several reasons, which for want of space and time I cannot mention here, there has been a systematic decay in everything and along side with it the women too have had to suffer their lot. Pardon me for saying that the condition of women nowhere in this world is as it should be. In straight forward language no one has suffered as much as the beloved at the hands of the lover. Judaism or Christianity have not been able to achieve much. In fact religion can't succeed much in matters purely concerning society. The society must evolve some means to eradicate this evil and I am sure in time to come things will take a different shape. Patience is necessary, for all great undertakings require a good deal of sacrifice and time, but any way even an inkling of hope is essential at the outset! . . .   [14.2.1945]

Typical invitation to an 'At Home' (*purdah*) afternoon, January 1945.

We began another rather lengthy tour on 1 February 1945. The party consisted of Sir Thomas, Lady Rutherford, Robin Cameron ADC, Dennis Crofton, the governor's secretary, and me.

We began our tour by crossing the Ganges and boarding a train to Chapra, where Lady Rutherford and I visited hospitals and *purdah* women. Also on this tour we visited Hattiwa, arriving in the early evening. We were met by the Maharajah and drove to his palace to stay in the guesthouse, which was well appointed. That night we dined with the Maharajah and others at Government House. The following day I roamed about the palace grounds taking pictures. The palace and the grounds were most impressive. The guesthouse was a large white building surrounded by a beautiful garden and the palace like those in fairytales with masses of colour and flamboyancy. We met the old Maharani who was dressed in a beautiful silver and gold sari. She gave both Lady Rutherford and me fine shawls made from cashmere and wool.

After lunching in the guesthouse, we drove to Gopalpanj for Sir Thomas to open the 'Grow More Food Exhibition' and for Lady Rutherford to do the usual round of visits.

That night we had dinner at the guesthouse before re-boarding the train and travelling on to Maharajganj. There we were met by Mrs Summers, wife of the director of Begg's Sutherland Sugar Factory, which served the many sugar plantations and provided important export income. We visited a sugar factory where we saw bullseyes and other confectionary being made and had large tins of sweets presented to us along with some Enos fruit salts, another product from the factory, and, I thought, an interesting addition to the bullseyes! Then it was once again to the train and off to Motihari. I remember Motihari because here we visited a female gaol that was full of murderesses, all of whom to me appeared harmless. We also went to a flower show, a committee meeting with speeches, and finally the girls' school.

There was essentially a routine to all our touring, although as we were always touring different towns, it was a wonderful way to see India and learn about the people and their culture.

Our next stop was Bettiah, arriving at some ungodly hour. While there, we visited hospitals and a knitting school, and took tea at the home of Mrs Ferris Munn. For a few days we stayed at Mrs Munn's guesthouse, set in a most delightful garden. During our time there, we enjoyed tennis at the local club, dining in the manager's bungalow and playing billiards. We also rode around very grandly in a carriage and pair with red-coated *chaprasis* riding in front and behind and visited the senior girls' school where we saw a play produced by the students. And one afternoon we had a most thrilling shoot on elephants – and I shot a hog deer and a pig!

The Maharajah of Darbhanga

We left by train for Darbhanga during the night. Darbhanga, a major city in North Bihar, was ruled by Maharajah Kameshwar Singh. The Maharajah was the largest landowner in India, a great industrialist and nationalist. He was born on 28 November 1907 and crowned Maharajah of Darbhanga in 1929, after the death of his father Maharajah Rameshwara Singh. He was nominated to the Council of States as the youngest legislator in India. He was also the youngest representative at the Round Table Conference at London in 1931. He remained a member of the Council of States until 1946, a member of the Constituent Assembly from 1946 to 1948, and a member of the Provisional Parliament from 1948 to his death in 1962.

The wealth of the Maharajah was immediately apparent. As our train left the main line, we passed through imposing gates and drew in at the Maharajah's private siding. A fleet of Rolls Royces, Bentleys and Mercedes

The Maharajah of Darbhanga on his throne with his Sam Brown sword and resplendent in his jewels. (Kalyani Foundation, Darbhanga)

The Maharajah of Darbhanga with his brother,
Raja Bahadur Vishveshwar Singh. (Kalyani Foundation, Darbhanga)

TOP: The Maharajah of Darbhanga's European guesthouse, where I stayed.
ABOVE: The Maharajah's Administration Offices. (Kalyani Foundation, Darbhanga)

met us, as well as the most beautiful looking carriages drawn by white horses for the servants and luggage.

The palace grounds were picturesque, consisting of two large palaces, swimming pools, artificial lakes with fish, and the guesthouse, which was surrounded by gardens and lawns.

The Maharajah's brother, Raja Bahadur Vishveshwar Singh, and Raja Bahadur's son, Tukku, met us on our arrival. Tukku was fourteen years old and looked handsome in his colourful turban and possessed the most beautiful and easy manners. The European guesthouse was surrounded by an artificial moat and was a small palace in its own right. I had my own sitting room, dressing room, bathroom and an enormous bedroom all in pale blue. The furniture was quite modern and not very attractive, but it was comfortable. I was given a puppy by Raja Bahadur – it was a springer named Mary, which I changed to Merry.

After a delicious lunch we went off to see the stables. Everyone played polo including young Tukku. The stables were more luxurious than most country houses. There were eighty ponies and more than 150 *scyces* to look after them. Everything was beautifully kept and every stall fitted with an electric fan. There were dozens of carriages of every description, including an elephant carriage in silver and gold. I went over to the administration offices in a grey Bentley, while Lady Rutherford travelled in the stunning blue Rolls Royce with the Maharajah. The offices were as big as the British provincial secretariat at Patna, and here the affairs of Darbhanga were managed. There were three palaces and five guesthouses in the complex, and all surrounded by immaculate gardens. I felt as if I had been transported to another world.

We visited Maribihir the next morning and tended to the business of the tour. This included speeches and a visit to a girls' school, where we sat out a performance in Hindi with the audience talking more loudly than the actresses. Afterwards we lunched at the old palace with one of the Maharajah's brothers, who gave me a cheque for 10,000 rupees to give to Sir Thomas for soldiers' welfare. That night we dined as guests of Raja Bahadur. It was a magnificent dinner, and I was seated between the Maharajah and Mr Ansorge, the Chief Secretary of Bihar.

A particular treat was driving to a local hospital at Laheria Sarai in the Maharajah's Victoria carriage, which had been built for the Prince of Wales. We had gaily dressed coachman and two outriders carrying lances on glorious horses and four behind. We felt thoroughly regal. The Maharajah had a state dinner in honour of Sir Thomas and Lady Rutherford in the large palace that night. As we approached the floodlit palace that evening a fountain in front turned on, lit from below by coloured lights so the spray appeared all green, red and orange like jewels.

Inside, the palace was ablaze with light from enormous chandeliers. The Maharajah's chair was red plush velvet and silver, with ivory sides

ABOVE: Interior of Throne Room, Palace of Maharajah of Darbhanga.
(Kalyani Foundation, Darbhanga)

and arms. We had a grand meal and afterwards retired to the ballroom where we watched movies. The walls in the dining room were painted from top to toe with scenes of dancing girls. The Maharajah told me at dinner that he was particularly proud of the paintings and surprised me by telling me it was painted by an Australian artist, who charged by the foot! There was a rich Australian artist somewhere out there.

One day at lunch the Maharajah asked me if I would like to visit his vaults and see his jewels. His jewels were acknowledged as the third best collection in the world and included Marie Antoinette's diamond necklace. He escorted Lady Rutherford and myself with his retinue of guards towards another area of the palace where large and heavily secured doors were opened to an unbelievable world: jewel-encrusted turbans, one with diamonds and pearls so heavy the Maharajah could wear it for only half an hour at a time, a Sam Browne belt encrusted with precious stones, a sword sheath encrusted with precious stones, and a sword on top of which sat the great Moghul emerald, the largest carved emerald in the world and originally belonging to the Moghul emperor on which a verse of the Koran was carved. There were tables with trays full of unset diamonds, emeralds, rubies and other precious stones. When I held up a seven-strand necklace of pearls almost down to my ankles, with the largest pearl almost the size of a pigeon's egg, I asked, 'Oh, when do you wear this?' He replied in some surprise, 'Oh that is not for me. It is for my ceremonial elephant.' I was reminded of the comment made to Maie

RIGHT: Jewels from the collection of the Maharajah of Darbhanga. *Top to bottom:* 1. Father Pink Diamond Ring; 2. Jehangiri Necklace; 3. Coochbehar Pearl & Diamond Necklace; 4. Coochbehar Necklace (Kantha); 5. Coochbehar Tawker Emerald Necklace; 6. (*right*) buttons; 7. (*left*) ring box. (Kalyani Foundation, Darbhanga)

BELOW: Jewels from the collection of the Maharajah of Darbhanga. *Left to right:* 1. Jancoo; 2. Big Head Ornament (Hamilton Jeega); 3. Nezamat Necklace. Bottom: Jewelled Sword. (Kalyani Foundation, Darbhanga)

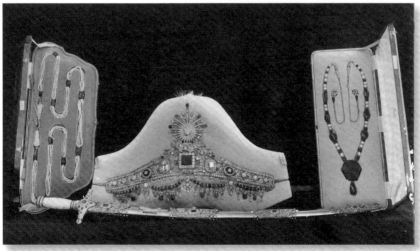

LEFT: Jewels from the collection of the Maharajah of Darbhanga.
Top (left to right):
1. Ruby, Emerald & Diamond Necklace (Murshidabad);
2. Teeka (Murshidabad);
3. Rubi Necklace (Murshedabad).
Centre:
4. Emerald & Diamond Kantha New.
Bottom (left to right):
5. Pahunchi;
6. Bhiybund.
(Kalyani Foundation, Darbhanga)

Casey by a friend who said, 'If you are going to India, don't take any of your jewellery because all the elephants will have so much better.'

The diamond necklace that had belonged to Marie Antoinette was a large cluster design of diamonds crossing from a diamond band that encircled the neck. When my fingers came in contact with it, I felt a chill run down my spine – I was literally holding history in my hand. The Darbhanga family had combed the world to assemble the finest collection of diamonds, emeralds, rubies, sapphires and great historical pieces. This was the India I had always imagined. Kameshwar Singh, who died on 8 November 1962, was the last Maharajah of Darbhanga, and I was privileged to be his guest and glimpse something of the lifestyle of this great family that, along with the jewellery collection, has now been consigned to history. The jewellery collection was split up following a property dispute between the Maharani and the Maharajah's nephews, and a large portion was sold in 1967. The Maharajah donated his palace for use as a university.

For part of this tour Tom accompanied us, having arranged to spend a week with me, and we were able to go on a shoot together. On this occasion we were guests of the Maharajah Bahadur of Darbhanga, along with other family members including Rai Baladur Singh of Bettiah, Raja Bahadur Viveshwara Singh, Darbhanga's brother, and his son Tukku. There was also a large party of Government House staff and visitors including Sir Thomas and Lady Rutherford, Tom and myself, Rudolph and Enid De Salis, Mrs Falkiner, Mr and Mrs Ferrons, Primus Munns, Mr P. Munro, and Francis Balfour. Lady Rutherford would put on her khaki slacks and pith helmet and she would sit and watch, either from an elephant or a *machan* in a tree. Our camp was in a delightful spot close to the Nepalese border, with a river running between us and the hills of Nepal. I described it as 'like something one sees in a film. There are wild monkeys hopping around and the prettiest birds I've ever seen'. [Diary, 7.3.1945]

The group went shooting the next day across the river into Nepal. Two tigers were seen during the first beat, but they escaped. The next day I was not feeling too well and stayed at the camp while the others went shooting and Tom finally shot a leopard. He wrote:

Went after a Leopard in am and I was in the beat. June stayed at home. I saw my first Samba, but could not persuade myself to shoot it. After lunch we went across the river for birds, pea fowl etc and put up two leopards. Raja Bahudur shot the first. The second gave a lot of fun and cost a lot of ammo. I thought I got it but without consultation it was awarded to Primus Munns. When on the way home we put up another. I finally got it at 60 yds with the rifle & it was given to me. A very exciting pm when not expecting anything.

Our tour then continued to Bettiah and then Murzzafarpur where I attended a wedding party in the home of Maharajah C.P.H. Singh with Lady Rutherford. We also attended a Red Cross party before returning to the train and proceeding on through the night to return home. We crossed the Ganges by small launch early the next morning, leaving the servants to cope with the luggage and follow later.

At one stage on our train journey home, the governor left to tour some of the province by car, to rejoin the train the next day further down the line. It was evening when we arrived at the station and there was a guard of honour, a band and much pomp and ceremony to greet him and escort him and his staff to waiting cars. The train then pulled out of the plat-form and we proceeded on our way. When we had got some way down the track, Tom's mad Afghan hound Boris jumped out of the window. Tom pulled the communication cord and the train came slowly to a halt. People came running down the line all screaming madly in Hindi. Tom yelled back 'Dog!' with lots of hand signs and the message seemed to get through, as the entire train was then backed to the station and people everywhere went looking for the dog. Boris was not found then, but later on and was given to the governor and duly returned in state in the vice-regal car! The thought of having an entire train backed to look for a dog seemed to me to show the power of the Raj.

Tom and Boris at the Darjeeling Hill Station, Bengal, 1945.

Tours was extremely tiring. Each was a public relations exercise where I was continually attempting to make polite conversation in a language that I was not familiar with. Yet each also held its own excitement and interest, especially the shooting expeditions, which were the preserve of the wealthy.

We returned to Government House in Bihar on the evening of 13 February and life returned to a measure of normality with office work, letters and thank you notes to write on behalf of Lady Rutherford to all the people we had met. I also had to make arrangements for the other activities in which she engaged. There would be many requests for her to attend functions, and I would need to reply to these after discussing it with her, so I did quite a lot of secretarial work. As proof of my usefulness I also gained some work from the military secretary at the request of Sir Thomas Rutherford when Francis Balfour's father fell ill and Francis returned to England. I now received 250 rupees a month, which came in very handy. It reached the stage in Bihar where I was practically running the household since Lady Rutherford was not interested in such things. She preferred using her time playing bridge and was devoted to her little Pekinese who was usually tucked under her arm. She even had me write letters to her friends on her behalf.

As mentioned, Lady Rutherford was a rather eccentric character and prone to speaking her mind, perhaps encouraged by her time in India. So diplomacy was not her strong suit. After we attended the wedding of Maharajah C.P.H. Singh's daughter, where staff from Firpos, the most famous restaurant in Calcutta, had undertaken all the catering, the Maharajah visited Ranchi and was invited to spend a night at Government House with us. During lunch when the Maharajah was telling Lady Rutherford something about what he called 'oonyans', she rather rudely corrected him. 'You must mean "onions", you don't say "oonyans".' He was very embarrassed and apologised, saying, 'Oh, your Excellency, I'm so sorry, your Excellency, so sorry.' In order to change the subject I cut in, 'Oh, your daughter's wedding was so wonderful. And that fish we had at the reception was absolutely fantastic, that beautiful spiced fish.' Lady Rutherford queried me, 'Did you think so?' and added, 'I thought it was terrible. Mine was nothing but bones.' I tried to save the day with, 'Well, I didn't get any bones at all.' Noel Shead, a rather amusing English captain of the Gurkha regiment and ADC, said, 'Well, maybe Lady Rutherford filleted the piece that June had.' The poor Maharajah who had beamed when I said how beautiful the fish was, was now suddenly crestfallen at Lady Rutherford's comment that she had nothing but bones. He got his own back, however, when truffles appeared on the menu. Lady Rutherford said rather condescendingly, 'Have you ever had truffles before?' 'Yes, your Excellency,' replied the Maharajah. 'And where was that?' asked Lady Rutherford somewhat haughtily. 'Here, yesterday,' came the reply. We all had to stifle our mirth.

On the other hand, Lady Rutherford's outspokenness could do much good. She and I visited the Patna hospital one morning and found the conditions in the operating theatres very uncomfortable. The rooms were stifling as there was no air conditioning. A wealthy Raja Bahada came to lunch with us at Government House that day and Lady Rutherford said to him, as though conferring an honour, 'Now you can give an air-conditioned operating theatre to the Patna Hospital.' 'Oh, thank you very much your Excellency, thank you,' came the grateful reply, and sure enough the Patna Hospital got a new air-conditioned operating theatre.

Protocol was always important within the Raj. I recall going to a small cocktail party and we did not want to leave too early thinking it would be rude to do so. We didn't realise, however, that everyone was waiting for the Government House guests to go before they departed. Protocol was particularly important to those in the Indian Civil Service and so no one would think of leaving a party until the most senior person had done so. I observed this on many occasions, and was the unwitting catalyst for one interesting example. I organised a party in my sitting room and invited Nancy, the Anglo-Indian wife of a High Court judge. She was extremely beautiful and I found her pleasant company, but none of the Indian Civil Service wives approved of her, because she was Anglo-Indian. They were very snobby and could be rather rude to her. My party went on interminably, with many of the wives becoming quite restive. I realised that Nancy, who had a habit of drinking heavily, did not look like leaving any time soon and none of the Indian Civil Service wives would leave until she had done so. By now it was clear they were ready to go and were merely standing around waiting. I went up to Nancy and said, 'You must go. None of them will go until you do.' She simply stood up rather shakily, looked around the room and in a loud voice said, 'Let the buggers wait,' and sat down!

Life in Bihar was enlivened by the arrival of the Rutherfords' daughter, Rhonda, in early March 1945, after she had completed her schooling in Melbourne. Rhonda was known as 'Plum' after her nanny referred to her

A dinner party hosted by me in my quarters, Ranchi, 1945.
Above: Lady Rutherford at far left, Maidie Falkiner, foreground.
Below: foreground, Lady Rutherford with her ever-present Pekinese.

as her 'little sugar plum' as a baby, and so became Plum for the rest of her
life. Mrs Norman 'Maidie' Falkiner accompanied Plum. She had been her
guardian in Australia. Maidie was the widow of Norman Falkiner who
had been one of Australia's leading and most progressive pastoralists and
racehorse breeders. Maidie was a large woman with snow-white hair and

the most beautiful and serene face. She had sparkling eyes, a wicked sense of humour, and was loved by everyone. Maidie's daughter, who married Major Stephen Blakeney, was living in Karachi, and her other daughter, Tempi Watt, was a close friend of mine, having frequently stayed with her when I was in Melbourne. The two had passed through Perth on their way to Bihar and brought up-to-date letters and news from my parents and friends. Both settled easily into life at Government House and proved a real boon.

Another thrilling experience was when one of the rich local *Zamindars* hosted a dinner in honour of Sir Thomas and Lady Rutherford, and I, as usual, accompanied them. The dinner was in the traditional Indian style, and we entered the dining area, where large cushions covered in rich brocade circled the floor and in front of each was placed a low table, also covered in brocade. We sat on the cushions and were served Indian delicacies and curries. The plates off which we ate were solid silver and entirely covered with fine engravings. To my incredulity, I discovered that the plates were used by Genghis Khan, the great Mongol emperor who

At Government House, Ranchi, 1945. *Left to right:* Noel Shead, Maidie Falkiner, me with my dog Merry, Rudolph de Salis, Lady Rutherford, Sir Thomas Rutherford, Tom, 1945.

brought them with him when he came on his conquering path through Asia, creating one of the greatest empires ever known and ravaging much of the country on his way, resulting in the deaths of forty million people. I sat there in wonderment trying to absorb the fact that Genghis Khan had eaten from these plates in the thirteenth century, and here I was eating from them in the twentieth century, 700 years later!

We went on tour again in March 1945.

With Tom

Life became less hectic when Tom joined me in Patna on 4 April 1945, partly as there was no longer the need for me to visit Calcutta at every opportunity. One of my last flying visits to Calcutta was on 31 March so we could celebrate our wedding anniversary together. It was not the intimate occasion we would have liked as Sir Renwick Haddow asked us to dine as a farewell to Tom before he transferred to Bihar. Also, before his departure, Leonard Aldridge approached Tom with the offer of a senior

LEFT: Playing tennis at Government House, Ranchi, 1945.
ABOVE: Tom riding at Government House, Ranchi, 1945.

position in his business empire after the war. Tom was flattered by the offer and promised to consider it, but gave no commitment. It would have meant us creating a life in South Africa. As a farewell, Richard Casey gave Tom a beautiful engraved silver cigarette case and invited us to stay at Government House whenever we were in Calcutta.

We were not altogether unhappy to be leaving Calcutta as a cholera epidemic was then spreading throughout the city.

The demands of life in Bihar were less onerous than those in Calcutta. One bright feature was the use of three horses provided by the Maharajah of Darbhanga on the understanding that we paid for their upkeep and returned them when we left. This meant that Tom and I went riding most days. We also played a great deal of tennis and squash and regularly went dancing at *Audrey House*.

We each had a dog while at Bihar, and overall there were eight different dogs belonging to the household, each dog having its own bearer. There was my springer, Tom's Afghan hound Boris, Lady Rutherford had a Dalmatian, a Pekinese and a Pomeranian and was looking after a Scottie and a dachshund, and Rudolph de Salis had a labrador. Each day before lunch we sat in a big room for drinks and there would be a procession of dogs – the little dogs first with small bowls and small bones, and as the dogs got larger so would be the bowls and the bones. The dogs would then be taken out on to the terrace where we could watch them being fed to be assured they got their food. On other occasions we sat out on the lawn in big cane chairs where crows would come swooping down to take the dog's food. Boris was very stupid and each day two crows would come down, one attacking him at the front and trying to bite his head while the other attacked his tail. Boris would turn around to snap at the crow attacking his tail and while he did, the other crow grabbed his bone. This happened every day and Boris never learnt. On the other hand, as soon as the crows appeared, the clever little Pekinese and Pomeranian picked up their bones and took them under the chairs and sat where the crows could not get at them or their bones.

CHAPTER 8

War's End

We attended a succession of parties and festivities celebrating the end of the war in Europe on 7 May 1945. There was a church parade on Sunday 13 May and a major military parade the following day. It was a spectacular show. There was also a rather a humorous side to it. When the Indian civil service, chiefs of staff, and others in their dress uniforms left from Government House to go to the parade ground, as many had not worn their uniforms since the beginning of the war and some had put on weight in the intervening years, they found it difficult to fasten their buttons. I remember hastily sewing on and repositioning many buttons before the official celebrations.

Tom was promoted to Major on 28 May 1945, which was news well received and duly celebrated. Not least it meant a raise in his pay. Given Tom's role, the constant visits of Lord Louis Mountbatten, and senior military men, we were able to follow closely the war in the Pacific. We immediately heard about the dropping of the atom bombs on Japan on 6 and 9 August and the official end of the war on 15 August. Peace was greeted with a sense of great joy and relief. Sir Thomas Rutherford assisted with the celebrations by giving a dozen bottles of both gin and rum to *Audrey House*. A thanksgiving service followed on Sunday 19 August.

Though the war in the East had ended, I still had plenty of work to do, having been given the task of furnishing all the recreation rooms in several of the army hospitals in Bihar. We girls also continued to dance with the troops at *Audrey House* when we were in Ranchi – with so few women around we had to go and give the soldiers a chance to have a dance. Also, not long after the war ended, we received as many as 1200 women and children internees who had been interned in Singapore. We frantically sought to find clothes, material for clothes, and toys. Many also required hospital treatment.

During my earlier rounds of the hospitals I had become quite chatty with a Major George Howard. He was very unhappy with his regulation army hospital pyjamas, so I got my *dhurzi* to make him some snappy pyjamas, monogram and all! At the same time, the Countess of Carlisle, senior controller of the Women's Auxiliary Service (ATS) and director of the Women's Advisory Council in India whom I had met in Calcutta, was staying with us at Government House in Ranchi. She mentioned that a cousin of hers by the name of Howard was in hospital somewhere in India and wondered where he was. On my hospital visit I asked my friend George Howard if he happened to be a relation of Lady Carlisle. As it turned out, he was the lost cousin. We had him brought to Government House to convalesce and Tom and I became good friends with him. I then discovered that he was the owner of the beautiful Castle Howard in North Yorkshire, England, where we visited him after the war.

There was, however, a sad intrusion into our Camelot. After being confined to bed for some considerable time, I miscarried for the third time since our marriage and lost a little son in spite of having been thoroughly spoilt with every possible attention. I had my lovely bedroom and

VE Day Celebrations, Ranchi, May 1945.
Tom in the foreground, Sir Thomas Rutherford in white uniform.

bathroom and my own balcony where I could recline looking on to the beautiful gardens of Government House. Apart from my own two servants, I had all the household servants to do any fetching and carrying I needed. I only had to press my bell by my lounge and one of ten *chaparasis* would come running to take my request for whatever I needed. I requested whatever food I wished and only moved from my bed to go to my bathroom. I went to the dining room about once a week and one night gave a cocktail party for Maidie Falkiner in my sitting room where I was able to just sit in a large chair and enjoy chatting to the guests. On another occasion, we had Sir Thomas and Lady Rutherford to dine with us in our quarters and had the Italian chef come in and cook the meal.

However, I made a quick recovery and we proceeded to get on with our everyday life. We had much to look forward to, planning our visit to England and France and then creating a home for ourselves in Adelaide after our long absence due to the war.

Lady Rutherford flew to Australia in late October 1945 for a six-week visit to make preparations for Sir Thomas's retirement the following May, after which the couple planned to live in Melbourne. This meant there was little pressure on me now, giving Tom and me the opportunity to plan our departure from India and our trip to Europe.

Many of our friends had started to prepare for life after the war – Gogo had already returned to America by the time of my birthday in March, with instructions from Tom and 450 rupees to buy me two evening dresses as my birthday present. John Pollington, Tom's predecessor in Bihar and now Earl of Mexborough, had invited us to stay with him, as had many of the friends we had made during our time in India. Once again, people in Perth became aware of our plans virtually as soon as we had made them. Priscilla Pepys of Perth's *Mirror* newspaper informed its readers on 15 December 1945:

CAUGHT sight of Shirley Perry homeward bound t'other day . . . Sister June who, before her marriage was one of Perth's most popular lasses, has been living in India, where I believe she has really been seeing life in its most sumptuous form, and meeting every one of note who, to ordinary people like myself, are merely famous names appearing in Press headlines. Very shortly, so I'm told, she will be leaving for England.

Everyone was on the move, with many heading for England. From all that we heard we believed we were going to freeze to death in the Atlantic, yet it was hard to buy appropriate clothing in India and everything was so expensive, so I made preparations of my own.

> We've bought a couple of Australian Army Blankets which are being dyed navy blue – and I'm having a dressing gown made for Tom and a Reefer coat for myself for the ship to wear with slacks etc. The quality of the wool is excellent in these Blankets, and they should make up well.
>
> [Letter, 26, 29.10.1945]

Organising our voyage to England proved more difficult than we had imagined because of the need to repatriate troops around the world. We had heard from shipping people that we could take a ship to Mombasa at any time, but had to receive priority to travel on to England, which we made sure to obtain before leaving India. Meanwhile, the first of my dresses bought for me in America by Gogo arrived. It was black, divinely cut and fitted beautifully, except that it was two inches too short and too slinky for me with a slit to the knee. Perhaps it was the influence of being so long with women who were shy of showing their faces that made me feel a bit bold having the slit as high as my knee. I arranged to have a good French dressmaker in Calcutta make an exact copy for me excluding the slit, and with the skirt softer in the front to suit me. The dressmaker agreed to make me another dinner dress in return for my dress and its pattern, which was worth something to her, so I felt I did quite well out of the deal.

We continued to meet people passing through Bihar from the war zone and hear some of the horrifying stories. One evening we went to tea to meet several former prisoners-of-war from Japan. One had been in the worst imaginable camp and so had lost his speech and the use of his legs. He was now able to walk a little and talked rather stutteringly. Another had suffered badly from ulcers and the Japanese were planning to amputate his legs as treatment. Fortunately, the Allies reached him before that happened and he recovered under the appropriate care.

We travelled from Ranchi to Patna in early November and began sorting all that we had gathered in India to prepare for our departure. This included the rugs made from the tiger and leopard Tom had shot.

The tiger skin had been sent to a firm called Van Ingham Van Ingham in Delhi, and I remember with amusement the letter back from them saying they had received the skin and asking us how would we like it mounted: 'With expression snarling or expression docile?' We naturally asked to have the tiger 'expression snarling'. We also had the good fortune to have Plum arrive on ten days' leave before she went to Japan, which meant we could bid her farewell.

Sir Thomas hosted a cocktail party in our honour on 10 November, a few days before we were due to leave Bihar, although we still had no idea when we would be leaving India or which route we would take. It seemed we would have to travel to East Africa, then travel from Mombasa to Nairobi, then to Lake Albert along the borders of the Belgian Congo and Tanganyika, then sail down the Nile to Cairo in a paddle-steamer. It certainly seemed like going the long way around if not adventurous!

We left Patna for the last time on 15 November on the overnight train to Calcutta to embark on our trip to England. We had been invited to stay at Government House, but chose to stay with 'Andy' Anderson. By this time the social unrest in India was worsening and we were glad to be leaving. One student riot left two police and a student dead, and over sixty people injured. There were riots and violence everywhere, particularly in Calcutta, and matters only worsened while we were there.

> Today they are patrolling the streets in bands and not allowing anyone to ride in rickshaws or Taxis and all trains are stopped. It's so humiliating to see taxis held up, and rickshaws and Europeans, including high ranking service people told to 'get out' — and more or less pushed out onto the street. There have been several ugly incidents around which we witnessed today — as soon as a car or rickshaw is stopped, in a second dozens and dozens of Indians have collected. Things are very sticky indeed . . .
> [Letter, 22.II.1945]

Another nasty episode occurred while we were in Calcutta, when students started rioting and were joined by others. One outbreak of rioting left thirty-three dead and 150 injured. We also learned that Carla Gordon, whom we had known in Patna, was on her way to the train when she was hauled out of her car and beaten up. She tried to defend herself by wielding a large thermos flask that we all carried, and was quite hysterical when she was found. We also learned of an American who was tied to his ambulance and burnt. Many local people were becoming rather insulting to non-Indians, and it was all becoming rather unpleasant. When we ventured out to try and arrange our travel, not surprisingly we preferred to walk, and happily we ourselves didn't experienced any trouble. But it was clear that the days of the Raj were sadly numbered.

Trying to find information about available shipping became our first priority. The Norwegian Consul said he had a ship leaving on 2 December, which would drop us in Antwerp. But as we were not in a position to make definite bookings for a few days, we had to relinquish the opportunity.

Most of our friends were not in Calcutta during our last visit, and while we occasionally dined at Club 300, it was not with the same jolly crowd as before.

Tom received his discharge from the army on 23 November 1945 after his final medical examination. He received six weeks' holiday with full pay and joined the ranks of the unemployed.

Having committed ourselves to go to England, we longed to be on our way, particularly because of the deteriorating social situation. We certainly wanted to ship our boxes out of India before the situation became chaotic and we lost the lot, so we arranged for them to go on the first ship to Australia. On 17 December we lunched at Government House and made our final farewells. We called on friends over the next few days, and had a final party at Club 300 with Andy and Boris the night before we were due to leave.

Our time in India had been magical. It was disappointing that the magic had dimmed during our last months there, and that the overall feeling in leaving was one of relief. Less than two years later, India became an independent nation in accordance with the plan devised by fellow dinner guest Lord Louis Mountbatten, which meant that we had been part of, and witnessed, the last days of the British Raj.

CHAPTER 9

Post-war Europe

We finally left Calcutta on the evening of 21 December 1945 aboard the 8000-ton Liberty ship MU *Samdel*, on our way to France and the United Kingdom. We had taken our luggage aboard in the morning to our two-berth cabin with a bathroom and a tiny deck that was more or less ours alone. Andy Anderson came down to the wharf and had a drink with us before we sailed, but he was the only one. There were not many of the old crowd still in Calcutta and those who were could not obtain a pass to come aboard or even visit the wharf, reminiscent of my departure from Fremantle. There were only two other passengers besides us, a Mr Fisher and a Mr Battison, so I was the only woman aboard.

After a month in Calcutta it was a relief to have no thought of riots and disturbances.

The *Samdel* had been built in September 1943 but had suffered during the war after being hit by a flying bomb. Liberty ships were so named because the United States of America had built the ships before it entered the war to assist Britain in carrying supplies and to replace ships that had been sunk by the German U-boats. They were cheap and quick to build and were meant to have a life of only five years. When we set sail on the *Samdel*, it was near its use-by date. During the trip we would hear on the daily radio news of yet another Liberty ship breaking up mid-ocean. After having been on board for only two days, we had our own scare when the ship nearly exploded. However, it was discovered in the nick of time that water was not flowing to the boilers, so the engines were quickly shut down and a terrific explosion averted. Engineers found an obstruction in one of the pipes which was soon fixed and we were on our way again, out into the Bay of Bengal and away from India. I had sailed to India in danger of being sunk by an enemy submarine and now I was leaving India in danger of suddenly sinking in mid-ocean! However, the *Samdel*, in spite of this ever-present danger and the boiler blowing up one night, delivered us safely to Le Havre.

Christmas Day 1945 was particularly memorable as it was the first one Tom and I had spent together despite having been married for nearly four years. We both had had great trouble getting to sleep on Christmas Eve as each of us was trying to stay awake after the other – for me to hang a stocking for Tom (which included a few small things he needed and some silver cuff links that I had made for him), and for him to bring out my present (which was cash to spend in England and France). The next day we had a lovely Christmas dinner with turkey and plum pudding and in the evening listened to the King's Speech and the Empire program. I also spent time sun bathing, which I did every day, and gained a great tan as well as studying French for life in France.

Our first landfall was Cochin Harbour (now Kochi) on 28 December 1945, a most picturesque place. The fishing fleet in the harbour comprised of locally made boats, constructed on the lines of ancient galleons, and upon entering the harbour, we noticed that on both sides were unusual fishing nets with claw-like suspension. Built around the harbour were fine-looking houses, which came right to the water's edge. We ventured ashore in the agent's rather snappy motor boat in the late morning, saw the prominent Malabar Hotel and then took a rickshaw and visited a mat factory. Afterwards, there was time for some shopping before returning to the ship, which remained at anchor in the middle of harbour. We spent the afternoon on board watching boys swim around the ship and dive for coins and bottles. This was the cleanest part of India I had seen. We went ashore again in the afternoon, swam in the hotel pool and had dinner there before returning to the ship late in the evening. We left Cochin the next day and settled back into our on-board routine.

New Year's Day, like Christmas Day, passed with the usual shipboard routine, although I remember it was very hot.

Life aboard the ship so far seemed rather repetitive – but that was all about to change. Tom complained of feeling ill and having a headache the day after New Year's Day, which we dismissed as the effects of too much sun. The next day, however, Tom became quite ill and developed a high temperature and was covered in horrid red spots with tops like water blisters. I was worried sick. As I later shared with my family back in Australia, we all immediately worried about smallpox, though we were afraid to say this out loud. There was no doctor on board so there was nothing we could do but wait until we arrived in Aden. All aboard were concerned about being quarantined. The constant heat made things even harder to bear, and eventually we put Tom's mattress on the deck because the cabin was too stifling.

We arrived in Aden in the early evening of 4 January 1946. We anchored in the harbour and hoisted the signal for a doctor. The doctor, when he arrived, was a wizened little Indian man who failed to instil confidence. We tried to explain that we thought Tom's spots might be the result of sunburn – which then led to a lengthy explanation of sunburn. When the doctor took one look at Tom from afar, in a frightened voice he said, 'Oh, I will go and get my colleague.' He was not game to get any nearer to the patient. Fortunately, the Indian sent for the port doctor, who was a charming young Englishman and, much to my relief, pronounced Tom to be suffering a severe case of chicken pox. The doctor departed after a beer or two and said we could continue the voyage and assured us Tom would be well again soon.

We were due to leave Aden early the following day, but before we did, the doctor came aboard with two others an hour before our scheduled departure to confirm his diagnosis of chicken pox and to reiterate that we were able to continue our voyage, but in quarantine.

The captain was not supportive. He sent for me early in the morning and lectured me because I had asked Joe Dickenson, the chief steward, for clean linen for Tom's bed. The captain said I could not expect clean linen every day, and gave me four sheets and said I would have to make do myself. When they were soiled I could soak them in Lysol and wash and dry them myself. He also informed me that I was to remain isolated with Tom and was not to go anywhere on the ship beyond our cabin and our small deck.

We finally sailed later in the morning after having to wait for some sleeping tablets for Tom. He and I were now quite isolated. The deck was roped off and everyone was told to avoid us. I had to clean the cabin and do our washing myself – which was quite difficult in a tiny cabin. Tom was not well at all, and I was sorry we had not stayed in Aden until he had recovered. He continued to worsen. I spent days sponging him, trying to make him cool and continually changing his bed sheets because of his severe skin reactions. The captain never bothered to enquire about Tom's health, even though his cabin was across the corridor. He was a perfect pig about it all and seemed to think we had done this on purpose. I was nearly dead with sleep deprivation, with all the washing and sponging and trying to make Tom comfortable, I had to wash and iron about five pairs of pyjamas a day!

Tom typically never complained and happily began to improve. The mate had been extremely kind and had done everything he could to make things comfortable for us. In fact, everyone except the captain had been very understanding. Even after Tom started to improve, the captain maintained his stony silence and declined to speak to me – he seemed to imagine that we purposely planned to bring an infectious disease on board. Meanwhile we were able to start enjoying the voyage again:

> Lots of islands around here – rather bare and grim looking places – just plain rock. About 5 pm came to the Sudanese coast and sailed along quite close. As the sun fell the coastline looked like something out of a picture postcard – Bare rocky mountains silhouetted against a hazy pinkish Eastern sky.   [Diary, 9.1.1946]

We arrived at Suez early in the morning of 10 January to a harbour filled with ships of various shapes and sizes. We arrived to considerable excitement, as the King of Saudi Arabia was arriving at the same time in his yacht, a glorious long white affair with gold scrolling at the bow and stern. As his yacht entered the harbour the escort vessel – *El Amir Farouk* – stood by and gave the royal salute. All the ships in the harbour were bedecked with flags and planes flew backwards and forwards overhead and a 21-gun salute was fired.

A doctor came on board and saw Tom, who was now well, although not looking particularly handsome with the remaining spots. We entered the canal in the early afternoon and passed a large French liner full of troops and service women. I found the canal to be rather uninteresting – the land on either side was a rather flat and dull-looking desert, with nothing as far as the eye could see.

We then travelled on to Port Said, arriving after midnight the following morning and leaving after about seven hours. At last we reached the Mediterranean, but sadly without the glorious sunshine we had hoped for. Tom and I were still in quarantine, so we had our meals on deck. When at last we were permitted downstairs, weather conditions had changed dramatically with freezing temperatures and blustery winds.

Though the war had ended, there were still reminders of it, which included dangers to shipping.

> Tuesday: Passed Pantellaria today – we have been going through known mine fields for nearly two days now and are approaching the worst of them – Hope there are no strays around!! Sea calmer today, although still fairly high and our progress has been slowed up somewhat. Passed Cape Bon, which was the last stronghold of the Germans in Tunisia. Quite close to the shores here – also passed Pantellaria very close. Could see small village tucked in among the hills.   [Diary, 15.1.46]

We steamed along the coast of Africa, the snow-capped hills an unusual sight in this part of the world. We passed Algiers at night, and were close enough to see the lights of the town. On the afternoon of 18 January we arrived at the Straits of Gibraltar. The Allies had heavily mined the Straits of Gibraltar during the war and they were just clearing a path for ships going through. We were blessed with beautiful weather and had an amazing view of the rock and of Sueta on the Moroccan coast opposite. But the beautiful weather was short-lived, and the following night we endured a terrific storm and awoke to find rain pouring into our porthole and the ship rolling and pitching madly. The loud claps of thunder and lightning, and the foghorn blowing, were far from reas-suring. The storm with its strong winds and high seas continued during the day and into the night, finally blowing itself out and the fine weather returning as we reached the Bay of Biscay.

European adventure

We arrived outside the French port of Le Havre in the late morning of 23 January. It was extremely cold and foggy and we could see very little. We passed several minesweepers on the job and heard a few mines exploding. As we moved into the port we sailed past scenes of complete devastation with large concrete pillars all around the coastline housing

German guns, now desolate and rusted. All the buildings along the sea front were in ruins. It was a pitiful sight – such a waste of human endeavour to build a city, only to have it laid flat on the ground in a mass of rubble.

We decided to go ashore even though no doctor had been to see Tom. The two other passengers, chief steward Joe Dickenson and Tom and I rugged up and trooped ashore in the early evening. The weather was bitterly cold. We tramped along the road and hailed the first vehicle that came along which was a truck. '*Parlez-vous anglais?*' I asked in my school French. '*Non*,' came the reply, so I started to speak in Hindi. All we could say was something sounding like '*Tecki-Salaane*' and '*Acha*.' We found it all rather amusing. The driver, who was a Yugoslav, gave us a lift as far as he was going. We then hailed a jeep and asked for a lift. After all piling in he told us he was a German POW. We suddenly had visions of him absconding with us and murdering us quietly somewhere – our fears by no means allayed by the fact that he drove at a terrific speed. We survived, however, and climbed out of the jeep at a cinema. By this time it was snowing heavily, although I enjoyed the sensation of the snow falling on my face.

The cinema was an American one and no women were admitted. Instead we were directed to a club a few blocks away. We arrived at a rather snappy American club called The Harbor Club and, as it was dance night, we were invited in and found the company most hospitable. There were large log fires burning, comfortable chairs, the latest magazines, a 12-piece band and hot coffee and doughnuts. There we met a Colonel Oliver and his English wife, as well as a Madame Lumiera – an English woman married to a Frenchman. The deputy port commander was also there. Since he knew where we were docked, he offered to take us back to the ship and arrange our passage on to England. Tom also met Colonel Robbins whom he had known in New Guinea, an amazing co-incidence indeed.

Back at the ship the captain remained cold towards us, determined to be rid of us at Le Havre. So the next day we went to the agent's office to arrange our forward journey. On our way, we met a friendly wharf labourer who spoke a little English, and we had a pleasant chat – he practising his English and us our French. We visited a bank and the post office where we tried to ring Madame Schiaparelli, Gogo's mother, to see if we could stay with her in Paris, but without luck, so decided we'd try our luck at finding accommodation when we arrived. At the railway station Tom obtained a military warrant to travel, and I purchased my ticket for travel to Paris the next morning. When we returned to the ship for lunch, we packed our bags and arranged to leave them with the agent during our stay in Paris.

I fell in love with Paris. The city was teeming with soldiers of every nationality and it was the first time I had ever seen prostitutes walking the streets. In fact, at night, one had difficulty in avoiding them in corners and doorways! We managed to spend time with Gogo and were lucky to have contacts like her and her mother in Paris, especially since we had trouble converting our Australian currency. Our travellers' cheques could be cashed, but not the letter of credit. So we had a tough time getting any money at all. We would have been unable to pay our bills had not Madame Schiaparelli come to our rescue. The lack of money prevented us from visiting Brussels as we had planned, so instead we stayed on in Paris and had enormous fun and went broke there! Gogo had a car so we spent a day at Versailles, touring the Palace and the Petit Trianon – a most divine miniature farm. For lunch we ate snails, which I found delicious, and ate several times again.

At the British Officers' Club in the city we were able to eat for a reasonable price, and we had many meals there. The club was in the house formerly belonging to the Baron de Rothschild, and was a combination of museum and pub. There were enormous marble statutes everywhere, colossal chandeliers and each room walled in brocade, a fabulous or precious material, or Chinese lacquer of exquisite panelling. There was a ballroom – previously a private cinema – where one could dance every night after dinner, and the bar was a long panelled room with beautiful carvings. We saw the Duke of Windsor on one of our visits to the club, and on one occasion, I stood next to him at the bar. We thought he looked quite old and grey, though Madame Schiaparelli later reported that he and his wife, Mrs Simpson, were particularly happy and he could not take his eyes off her for a moment. But apparently the Queen was quite firm about not having her in England.

We also spent a day at Fontainebleau. Martha Hyett from the American Red Cross, who was staying with Gogo, arranged for us to go on a Red Cross organised tour. We left the next day at 9.30 am with several American officers and drove to a tiny village called Brabazon, a most picturesque place and the home of many past and present famous artists. We then had lunch at Fontainebleau and after went to see the Palace.

> They are quite fantastic these French Palaces (and old houses even), a mass of gilt, brocade and paintings. Fontainebleau was most inter-esting – and it's such a pity to think that the art of making such beau-tiful pieces of art as are in it, has been lost today, in this 'machine driven' world. The forest of Fontainebleau is beautiful. We drove right through it as one must to get to the Palace.   [Letter, 8.2.1946]

We dined several times with Madame Schiaparelli and Gogo accompa-nied us everywhere. We attended the Opera Comique, heard the *Barber of Seville* after our day at Fontainebleau, and later went to the Opera House to hear *Samson and Delilah*. I wrote home that:

> It was magnificent . . . the Opera House is quite wonderful. It also amused me the way one sips champagne in between acts. It all seems so luxurious and expensive (and is!!) but the typical attitude of these people seems to be one of 'wine, women and song'.   [Letter, 8.2.1946]

We did not relish the idea of returning home and drinking champagne only as a luxury after our time in Paris, where we drank it instead of water! We gathered in the Ritz Bar, or one like it, every evening at about 6 pm and drank champagne before dinner. The city was virtually closed from Saturday to Tuesday each week and it was impossible to achieve anything on those days. Even the Louvre and other noteworthy tourist places were closed. Nevertheless, we found time to visit Napoleon's Tomb, which made me wish I had taken more notice of my history lessons, so inspired me to read history books again. I did not do much shopping because of our money shortage and the cost of everything, but I did buy two woollen dresses, which were both quite plain, but the only ones I could see that would be practical for me. They were also inexpensive as they were being sold off at the end of the season at the Salon Schiaparelli.

On our last night in Paris we visited a very snooty place called *The 40*. Gaining admission was normally very difficult, but Gogo was able to make the necessary arrangements. I wore a green crepe dress that I had made in Calcutta, which was a raging success. Thanks to Gogo, we sat at the 'Royal Table' with the fourth member of a group a French airforce colonel who insisted on paying the bill. Afterwards Gogo told us he had 'oodles of cash', so we didn't argue too heartily about it!

We returned to Le Havre and stayed at a quaint hotel and the only one left standing. The Americans had requisitioned it and had booked us in there prior to the sailing of the *Huntingdon*, on which they had been good enough to arrange our passage from Paris to England. I was at breakfast one morning before we sailed when an American soldier about to return home approached me and asked, 'You're about to go to England, aren't you?' 'Yes,' I replied. He responded, 'Would you do something for me?' I said, 'Yes, depending on what it is.' 'Take this,' he said, 'and do what you would like with it. It is no good to me.' He then gave me £500. I was rather stunned and when Tom joined me I said, 'We've just been given a present. We now have some money when we arrive in England.' Tom said, 'What on earth have you been doing since I left you?' I think he may have imagined some French habits had rubbed off!

The trip to Southampton was in an American supply boat, so we stayed in a little cabin full of packages. From Southampton we took a train to London where we arrived on the afternoon of 14 February. The effects of the bombings in London remained evident everywhere. The debris had been cleared away, and temporary walls and hoardings had been erected around the badly damaged sites awaiting remediation. Tom's great-uncle, Fred Clendenning, was happy to have us stay with him in his flat in St John's Wood, not far from Marble Arch. Uncle Fred was a very old-world person, straight-laced and had lived in China during the Boxer Rebellion.

We met several friends from India soon after our arrival. I rang Enid de Salis the day after we arrived to arrange a meeting. We also saw George Howard in London and later went to visit him at Castle Howard.

We spent a great deal of time in London and did the usual tourist things, including a visit to Windsor Castle. We saw Eton, lunched in Nell Gwynne's house, saw the chapel and castle, and had tea with Lord and Lady Gowrie. Lord Gowrie had been the Governor-General of Australia and his son, Patrick Hore-Ruthven, who had been killed during the war, had been a friend of Tom's. I went to an 'At Home' at Lady McCann's. Lady McCann was the wife of the South Australian High Commissioner. We also lunched with Arthur Penn, the Queen's secretary, who was a great friend of Enid's, and who took us to see the royal stables at Buckingham Palace.

We made our first venture outside London with a visit to Oxford by train with Enid. It was exciting for us to have our first glimpse of this old, quaint town, with tiny crooked buildings with minute doors and windows.

Tom managed to buy a new Hillman car and find sufficient petrol so we travelled all over the country and visited many of the friends we had made in India. We travelled through Colchester and went on to Suffolk. We went to the tiny village Bury St Edmunds, then attended a dinner party given at a pub called The Bull at a town nearby called Long Melford. We then drove from Suffolk to Sandringham in Norfolk, to see the King's farms where Captain Fellowes, to whom we had had an introduction, took us all over the place before we travelled on to Cambridge. In Cambridge we toured the colleges and later dined with Tom's relatives, the Brookes, who we were unable to stay with because of the bomb damage to their home.

Gogo and Berry Berenson travelled from Paris for a one-day visit to see us in London on 15 April. We dined at Quaglinos restaurant and then went to the 400 Club, one of London's posh nightclubs. Also during our stay in London we lunched at Claridges with Enid and Rudolph de Salis, who had arrived that morning.

Fortunately, we had the opportunity to see the first performance of the Royal Ballet after the war. It was a Royal Command Performance at Covent Garden in which Robert Helpmann was cast as the wicked fairy in *Sleeping Beauty*. Tom had known Robert, or 'Bobbie', in Adelaide prior to the war and he was able to obtain seats for us. Afterwards, we went to his dressing room to see him, and the scene that confronted us became indelibly printed on my memory. Bobbie was dressed in a big black witches hat and black flowing robes. His dresser entered and Bobbie began putting on a tantrum screaming, 'I must have jet earrings, I must have jet earrings!' and swishing around his little dressing room as he did so, knocking things off his dressing table.

Later, we travelled to Salisbury. On our way we stopped at several quaint villages in the area where Tom had been when he was camped at Salisbury during the early war years. We stayed at an attractive pub called the Red Lion in Salisbury, which had an old coach house and cobbled courtyard. Salisbury Cathedral was one of the most beautiful I had seen.

> We lunched at another old pub called 'The Haunch of Venison' then drove on . . . to the Harbens – They are only 7 miles from S'thampton in fact from where we are sitting now on the terrace we can see the Docks, as the house is high on a hill. It is a most lovely place, with a glorious garden (6 gardeners and they say they're understaffed!) The house is beautiful and so luxuriously comfortable – all oak panelled down-stairs – with lovely paintings and works of art in it. It's so lovely to relax here in the sunshine . . .
>
> While I'm sitting here I can hear the Cuckoo quite plainly – the first time I've heard one. It's such a perfect Spring day and the country is unbelievably lovely. Tom has just gone off on a bike [bicycle] to accompany Phyllida aged 11 who is on her pony and is going to tea with lots of other small girls and their ponies . . . She had to go along the Main Rd. a bit, so Tom has gone to see her safely there. She's got a darling pony and looks so sweet going out in her jodhpurs and little velvet cap. [Letter, 19.4.1946]

Our next stop was Portsmouth, then Winchester, as well as stopping at several places in between. Gradually, we wound our way back to London. We then stayed in Kent with Enid and Rudolph de Salis before heading north to Birmingham. We crossed into Ireland on 14 May and had great luck being able to stay at the The Royal Marine Hotel at Kingstown, which was the port of Dublin. We were not able to book any accommodation beforehand, but found the hotel to be comfortable and the meals good, although we only ever ate breakfast there having decided to visit different places in Dublin for each meal. The plentiful food that was available made us realise how monotonous the food was in England. We travelled to Killarney then returned to Dublin via Mallon, Carlow and Kilkenny, which we found a much prettier trip than the one through Limerick.

I had set aside 23 May, the day before we were due to return to England, to do my shopping. This was a disaster! While trying on the coat of a suit in the first shop I entered, someone 'lifted' my handbag and walked off with it. I had only left it there a moment while I tried on the coat, and when I went to pick it up before walking over to the mirror it had vanished. My passport and everything was gone and we were due to leave for England early the following morning. I spent the remainder of the day at the police department and the passport office. I wasn't able to get a new passport, but was provided with a letter to give to the immigration authorities saying who I was and had to hope this would be enough to get me into England! Fortunately, my bag was found at a pork and beef shop two blocks from where it was stolen, and apart from taking my money, all else was intact.

On the move once more, we crossed to Holyhead then drove to Stoke through North Wales and on to the relatives of Tom – Ben and Adele Brookes – who lived at Childerley Hall, near Cambridge. Childerley Hall had a room at the top of the house, known as the King Charles Room, as Charles II, when being brought down from Scotland by Cromwell's forces, was held there overnight before being taken on to London for execution. I commented that all the oaks in the grounds of Childerley Hall seem to have large calluses around their trunks about three feet from the ground with the main branch growing up from there. Ben explained to me that when King Charles was executed, all loyalists lopped the heads of their oaks in a show of sympathy for the King, and the trees grew from this. This was the reason for them being misshapen, and they are now known as 'King Charles oaks'.

We also called on George Howard at Castle Howard near the City of York, who by now had returned home. Castle Howard became renowned, as it was and later featured in the film *Brideshead Revisited*. It had been used as a hospital during World War II and had not yet been restored to its former grandeur. We found George living in the wing that housed the kitchen. George later became head of the BBC and an influential businessman in England.

Back in London we had a hectic social life. One night began with a dinner party at Grosvenor House, then on to a ball and from there to meet Laurence Pratt at the Orchid Room, a trendy nightclub. As we were so late in leaving the ball, after transporting Pam Hore-Ruthven and Johanna Curzon to their respective homes, we decided it was too late to continue the party so called in at the Orchard Room simply to tell Laurence that we were going straight home. We began talking and, when we finally decided to leave, found that it was daylight. Someone then suggested that we have breakfast before going home. So Laurence, Tom

and I, a South American, and three chorus girls of various nationalities –
two of whom were tipsy and leaned on Tom for support – went to Mr
Lyons Corner House for breakfast, looking like a circus. We finally made
it home at 6.30 am to be met by old Uncle Fred in his pyjamas. I think
he wanted to check that we hadn't had too much to drink and was very
disappointed to find us stone cold sober!

The four days of the Ascot Racing carnival were particularly gruel-
ling. We had an easy first day there but finished the second day with an
all night party and dance. We again stayed the course till dawn, had our
photograph taken at 7 am, and then returned to our hosts for breakfast.
Afterwards we drove back to London, changed clothes, and proceeded
back to Ascot. After parking our car in the Duke of Norfolk's private
garage, 'We sallied forth in great style and had a picnic lunch in Windsor
Great Park on the way.' The Royal Procession was the highlight of the
day for me.

> They come down the track in front of the Stand, in the lovely open
> carriages with outriders and footmen dressed in gold and scarlet. As
> it was inclined to rain the outriders, coachmen, etc all wore their rain-
> coats, which are bright scarlet and look so grand. It was a wonderful
> sight, and as they drew up and got out I was almost close enough to touch
> them.   [Letter, 24.6.1946]

On the only other day that the weather was fine enough for a procession, the Duchess of Kent and Princess Mary were also there. The women
were all dressed very smartly.

> I looked frowsy which spoiled things a bit for me – but it's no use
> worrying as unless I pay about £50 & wait 12 months I haven't a hope –
> & then I can't get things to match. I'm just one big mess! The weather
> spoilt things as everyone started off in flowery hats & pretty dresses then
> it started to pour. So they had to wear coats & change into dull hats. It
> was terribly muddy too – & ones feet got sopping. Girls in white toeless
> shoes were mud up to the ankles.   [Letter, 24.6.1946]

That night, being Uncle Fred's eighty-eighth birthday, we took him and
his friends, the Harbens, to the Savoy for dinner. The old boy was thrilled to
pieces and asked the band to play a Strauss waltz, and waltzed me around

the floor, which was not bad at his age. As we were leaving about an hour after midnight, Fred said, 'My dear, I've never seen one of these night clubs they talk about.' So we took him to the Orchid Room. We asked the band to play 'Happy Birthday' and when we told them why, they would not believe us until they saw him sitting there beaming. They said, 'Boy, we'll play *anything*,' and sang 'Happy Birthday Uncle Freddie,' in swing time! Old Freddie beamed away at everyone. When we got home a couple of hours later, I brewed some tea and fell into bed. Feddie was up as gay as a lark only three hours later! I think he thought it the best birthday he had ever had. We eventually got ourselves up to attend the final day at Ascot.

We left London again on 24 June and headed to Scotland, attending the first day of the open golf championship at St Andrews.

We once again returned to London where we were guests at a garden party at Buckingham Palace. This was the first such party hosted by the King on a large scale since the war, but nevertheless it was something of a dreary show.

As in India, we found difficulty in making definite arrangements to return to Australia. We made our wish known at Australia House, but had to wait our turn for an available ship. We eventually gained passage aboard the *Sarpedon*, which set sail for Australia via South Africa on 3 August 1946. We had a comfortable cabin, though not luxurious. A significant fellow passenger was the Irish ambassador Dr T.J. Kiernan who, with Mrs Kiernan, was making his way to Australia to take up his appointment. On our journey we called in at Cape Town and Durban, and then had a very slow journey across the Indian Ocean because of industrial action by the stokers on board who refused to maintain steam. We would go racing through the ocean when the boilers were stoked and then gradually get slower and slower and grind almost to a halt until the next crew of stokers arrived. Because we were finally headed for home and anxious to get there, we did not want this sort of disruption.

I had experienced France and England for the first time, but soon we would have to settle back into a less exotic civilian life when we returned to Australia. It was 1951 before we were able to return to England, but we did so virtually every year afterwards, where we were lucky to have so many friends and to stay in their beautiful homes, many of whom also came and stayed with us in Adelaide.

CHAPTER 10

Return to Reality

Our time and experience in India had left us with memories that would remain with us forever. As well, we had been fortunate to see Paris and travel in England, Ireland and Scotland on our way home. But now there was the business of planning the rest of our lives.

We returned to Australia aboard the 11,321-ton Blue Funnel Line *Sarpedon*, arriving in Fremantle on the morning of 15 September 1946. We were met by my parents, Marjorie Learmonth, who had returned to live in Perth after Charles had been killed, and our old family friend Leslie le Soeuf, who had commanded the 2/7th Medical Division and been taken a prisoner-of-war in Crete. He had bravely stood up to the Germans and received better conditions for his POW men. He and Marjorie married the following year. We stayed with my parents for a brief time, giving us the chance to catch up with my old Perth friends, including Robin Cameron whom I had last seen in India.

On our return to Perth, September 1946 (photograph *West Australian*).

On our return to Adelaide we stayed at the South Australian Hotel for as yet we had no home of our own. Tom's family home, Cosford, had been let during the war and Tom's mother had moved out to rented accommodation before going to live with Arthur on his farm at Apsley in country Victoria. We too were looking to make our new life in the country on the farm at Penola. However, after a family discussion, the consensus was that one member of the family should stay in town and look after family affairs. Both of Tom's brothers were settled in the country now, with Arthur acquiring his property at Apsley after being invalided out of the army. He later married Jane Baylis, the daughter of Denis and Esther Baylis of Binnum in April 1948.

The decision to remain in Adelaide was not what we had expected or hoped – I wanted to live in a home of our own rather than the Porter family house. But after much discussion, it was decided that we should move into Cosford. Excluding the war when Tom's mother had moved out, the Porter family had lived at Cosford continuously for three generations. Still, during the war years the house had been difficult to maintain, and so a great deal of work was required to make Cosford 'home' again. While the work was being carried out, we took a flat in Frome House, on the corner of North Terrace and Frome Street.

Tom's broking business F.W. Porter and Company had come to a halt while Tom was in the army and overseas, so on our return, Tom's uncle Sir Collier Cudmore, offered the use of a tiny room in his law office. With his secretary, Miss Barter, Tom recommenced trading as F.W. Porter & Co. Miss Barter, known affectionately as 'Barty', was a large woman and with her, Tom, and goodness knows what else in that office, I don't know how they managed to squeeze in. Tom soon found an office in Grenfell Street where he remained as he expanded the firm.

Once again, Tom and I were to know great grief when I miscarried for the fifth time, our little son living for only three days. With today's modern technology this would have been avoided, but in the 1950s no hospital in Adelaide possessed a humid crib. Our little bundle struggled for life at the foot of my hospital bed in a cradle, over which was attached a wire hoop covered with wet towels with a light bulb suspended overhead to try and create some humidity. On the third morning I was awakened at 3 am and found Tom framed in the doorway of my hospital room with a ghastly forced smile on an ashen face. 'What on earth are you doing?' I asked. 'Just going for a walk,' he replied. 'What! At this hour of the morning?' He then came over to my bed, held my hand tightly, and told me that the hospital had rung him at home with sad news. My immediate thought was 'Oh, poor Tom. He was so looking forward to having a son. He will be heartbroken.' But I knew that his thoughts were only for me. We both grieved for each other, but in spite of our grief we recognised how much good fortune we had in life, and above all we had each other. We realised that if we were not to have the family we would have liked, we were lucky to have lovely nieces and nephews, all of whom became a great part of our lives. Few people are not touched by grief at some time during their life, but life is for living, not grieving, and one must get on and live it. Yet no matter how deeply one's grief is buried it is always there. All these years later I have to close my doors and windows to block out the sound of the peal of the bells of St Peter's Cathedral when there is bell practice on Tuesday night, as it brings memories flooding back from that time when I was in the hospital near to the Cathedral. Even to this day I sometimes have nightmares and wake up crying.

After eventually managing to effect the necessary renovations to Cosford, Tom and I were ready to begin our lives in the large Victorian villa of twenty rooms set on more than a hectare of land. The garden had also been neglected during the war and was now completely overgrown, so we brought in eleven sheep to eat the weeds down on the tennis court. Just as I was leaving to meet Tom for a cocktail party one evening, I had a telephone call saying, 'There are sheep in Hawker's Road, would they be yours?' So I hastily scrambled down to Hawkers Road in my best party clothes to round up the escaped sheep. It seemed a far-flung excuse for being late for a cocktail party, to say that I was rounding up sheep in suburban Adelaide!

Another problem in such a large garden was the number of snails, so we acquired three Indian runner ducks that we named Winken, Blinken and Nod, to rid us of them. They were so effective, that having run out of our snails, they ate all the fish in the pond and then waddled across the road to clean up the snails in the neighbours' gardens. It soon reached the stage when we had to feed them. When I was Lady Mayoress, people motoring along Edwin Terrace some evenings were surprised to see me, fully booted and spurred ready for an official event, standing in the middle of the street loudly calling, 'Quack! Quack! Quack!' after which three ducks would appear from a garden in the street, waddling in line across the road. Winken, Blinken and Nod sadly found a bucket in the stables that had some of the pre-Winken, Blinken and Nod snail killer in it and I fear that was their last supper. Divine retribution!

Having done a great deal to tidy the house and the minimum renovations in deference to Tom's mother, we discovered that the house had actually belonged to Tom the whole time. Before his father died he had expressly wished that Tom should live there. So Tom, after discussing this with his brothers, arranged that they should each get a third of the value of the house toward their own homes, and Cosford became ours.

Life at Cosford

The land on which the home stood meant we had ample space for Tom's polo ponies as well as a menagerie of chickens, ducks, pheasants and partridges. We exercised the horses every morning before breakfast, often startling motorists as we rode down Northcote Terrace to the park lands. I did much of the gardening myself after we moved in, since it was difficult to get skilled help. I did, however, have the help of a gardener named Ashenden, who was quite a character and whose family had worked for three generations of the Porter family. But this familiarity meant that he did whatever he wanted in the garden. I remember on one occasion giving him masses of white petunias to plant, and being surprised when the garden became ablaze with red petunias. On mentioning this phenomenon to Ashenden, he simply said, 'Don't like white flowers,' and walked away. Later, we had an Italian gardener, Alberto. Nobody could understand Alberto's broken English but he and I had a wonderful working relationship, as I seemed to make sense of his mumbo jumbo and he seemed to understand me. He stayed with us until I moved out, and then stayed on with the new owners. I later also had live-in help in the house, which included some wonderful people who stayed with us for many years.

Cosford was a big house meant for entertaining and the house was always full of people. We had formal dinner parties, garden parties under

RIGHT: Cosford.

BELOW: The garden.

CAN A DUCK SWIM?

Cosford, 1951. TOP: exterior; the stables; MIDDLE: dining room; smoke room; BOTTOM: rose garden; terrace under oak tree and tennis court in background. OPPOSITE PAGE: The front garden.

144

the oak tree and many fundraising events. Friends from Europe and inter-state also came to stay with us. Cosford also remained the Porter family home where all the members of the family congregated at Christmas. Arthur's two sons and two daughters attended boarding schools in Adelaide, and would stay with us on weekends, regularly inviting their friends over as well to visit and play tennis or billiards. The tennis court was in continuous use during the summer months. I had women's tennis on Wednesday, Tom had men's tennis on Saturday when he was not playing polo and we had mixed tennis on Sundays, after which everyone invariably stayed on for drinks.

Tom took on an increasingly public profile as we settled into Adelaide, and I began working for several charities such as the Girl Guides, the Crippled Children's Association, the Red Cross and the Australiana Fund, which Tammie Fraser started when Malcolm Fraser was Prime Minister. At various times, Tom served as president of the Good Neighbour Council, was president of the RSPCA, a member of the Council of the Royal Zoological Society, a member of Legacy, a governor of the Anti-Cancer Foundation and a member of the Council of the St John Ambulance Brigade. Tom acted as Consul for Belgium from 1953 until his death, and received honours for his time spent in this role, including his appointment as a Chevalier of the Order of the Crown and as a Knight of the Order of Leopold. The task was not onerous but involved paperwork and attend-ance at formal occasions. All this meant that I became involved with these organisations too and was kept very busy.

Tom on one of his polo ponies, and inset, a Frank Lees caricature of Tom.

Tom continued to play polo after we returned to Adelaide and was one of the chief movers in relocating the club to a property at Waterloo Corner in 1960. The long time polo grounds at Birkalla in West Torrens that had served the club since 1902, had become surrounded by urban subdivisions leading to an increase in rates, which the club could not sustain. Selling Birkalla provided enough money to purchase Waterloo Corner, establish a new polo ground and centre, yet with money left over to invest in the club's future. Tom also continued his involvement in rugby and served as president of the South Australian Rugby Union for ten years from 1949.

After travelling for so long, I was delighted to have my family close by. My sister Shirley travelled back and forth between Perth and Adelaide before establishing her interior decorating business in Adelaide, where she met her husband Bill Matthew. My parents also moved to Adelaide to be nearer Shirley and me, and lived in Smith Street at Walkerville, quite close to Cosford. My father had retired in 1946. He had always been involved and interested in politics, and had accompanied Robert Menzies when he travelled around Western Australia forming the United Australia Party. In 1947 he ran unsuccessfully as the endorsed Liberal candidate for the seat of Perth – a strong Labor seat – though he did manage to make considerable inroads into the Labor vote.

My father died at home on 15 October 1975. Sometime after, my mother was knocked over by a car while we were visiting Lizard Island, and broke both her legs. She recovered, but became dependent on a walking frame. Then not long after her accident, after sitting down to watch television, she had a heart attack and died peacefully.

Indian contacts

While concentrating on our life in Adelaide, we continued to follow the careers of several of our friends from our days in India, maintaining regular contact with many of them. Although we did not see Boris Lissanevitch again, we followed his career with interest. Club 300 in Calcutta continued after the war, though with Boris relinquishing his role as director in 1946. Soon afterwards, the King of Nepal invited Boris to Nepal, where he moved in 1951 and established the first international hotel there, featuring the Chimney Restaurant, which became as renowned as Club 300 and continued until 1961. He also created the famous restaurant Yak and Yetti, and opened one of the royal palaces to tourism. Boris's efforts did a great deal to open Nepal to foreign visitors. At one point, however, he seems to have created some misdemeanour and found himself in jail. Fortunately for Boris, the King of Nepal was about to be crowned and this ceremony required a crown of butter, and the only person in Nepal capable of producing this was Boris. Boris was released to do the job and achieved certain fame, and became a favourite of the royal family. Boris died in Katmandu on 20 October 1985, eighty years old.

Syd de Kantzow was another whose career we followed with interest. Syd, with American Roy Farrell who had also flown over 'the hump', hatched a plan to acquire surplus aircraft left behind by the United States after the war. In September 1946, they established a small airline which they expanded, and which eventually became Cathay Pacific. Angela May and Syd married and had a delightful son, Peter. Syd, who was on the board of Cathay Pacific, sold his shareholding in the company in 1951. Syd then came to live in Sydney with his family, where we visited them in their home overlooking the Harbour. Despite all Syd's dangerous air exploits, he died when going to see the new development of Thredbo in 1957, and the car in which he was a passenger went off the road and over the mountain. His son Peter and his American wife Stephanie and

Syd and Angela de Kantzow with their seaplane.

their two daughters went to live in Hong Kong, where I have visited them and had wonderful travels to Russia and South Africa with them. Peter, like his father, was also involved in aviation and became a co-founder of Waterfront Air, based in Hong Kong.

After a distinguished war record, Hilary Hook, another colourful character Tom and I had come to know well, continued to serve in the British Army in many of the world's trouble spots, retiring with the rank of lieutenant-colonel in 1964. He then went to Kenya where he managed a game farm and gained notoriety when, in 1988, he appeared in a BBC television documentary featuring his adventurous life. We corresponded for several years and despite making several attempts to visit him in Kenya, sadly something always intervened and we never made it. Ed Greever was another we were sorry not to have been able to see again.

But many of our friendships made in India continued for many years, though with travel not as accessible as it is today, it took longer to get around the world than one would have liked.

Tom also remained in contact with Sir Thomas Blamey. Sir Thomas had remained Commander-in-Chief until 1 December 1945, and spent his latter years writing and promoting the welfare of former service personnel. Five years later, on 8 June 1950, he was promoted to Field Marshal, and requested that Tom attend the Heidelberg Repatriation Hospital were he was confined and where Governor-General Sir William McKell presented him with his Field Marshal's baton on 16 September 1950. Tom found it very emotional, recalling that there was hardly a dry eye in the room. He described Sir Thomas sitting in bed in his Field Marshal's uniform, staring straight ahead not speaking to anyone. He died of a cerebral haemorrhage the following year on 27 May 1951.

We were sad to not have had more contact with Sir Thomas and Lady Rutherford, especially since they had returned to live in Australia when Sir Thomas retired. Lady Rutherford died on 8 April 1955 and Sir Thomas two years later. Although I did maintain contact with Plum – she was a brilliant girl and quite eccentric like her mother. Perhaps from her unsettled upbringing, Plum, misguidedly, felt concerned that prospective suitors were interested in her for her inheritance only. Happily she met Marty Haet, a young American doctor, in a swimming pool in Singapore and they fell in love and married. They had a beautiful home outside Los

Angeles where Tom and I visited them. They had two children together and felt they had so much happiness in life that they should give something back to society, so they joined President John Kennedy's Peace Corp and travelled to a South Pacific Island where Marty worked as a doctor and Plum assisted the community. They were having a picnic on the beach one day with their two little children and the nursemaid, when a freak wave swept them all out to sea. Plum and Marty were washed back but the children were not to be seen. Marty went back into the sea to try and find the children, who by this time had been returned safely to shore. He drowned while out looking for them. The children had never attended a regular school but had received a wonderful education by travelling the world with Plum, seeing other countries and learning many languages. Plum succumbed to Alzheimer's disease in her old age.

Our first opportunity to renew contact with British and European friends came when we travelled overseas in 1951. We saw Gogo Berenson, Rex Peel, and Tog – now Sir Francis Mellersh. We saw Gogo regularly for many years afterwards, and I stayed with her often after Tom died. Berry Berenson died of cancer, and after his death Gogo married Gino, an Italian marquis, and became the Marchesa de Cacciapuopti di Giugliano. I stayed with her in Paris and also at their home in Italy. She and Gino had a big house on the coastline near the town of Santa Margherita. The house was above a rocky cliff, with steps carved into the rocks that led down to the sea and a little kabana with a fridge and other conveniences. We would sunbake on the rocks and dive from them into the sea. A couple of years later when I was travelling with other friends on a yacht sailing in the vicinity, we anchored off Santa Margherita. I decided to have a bit of fun and swim ashore, saying, 'It would be rather amusing if Gogo and Gino are there having a swim and suddenly I rise out of the water like Aphrodite.' Unfortunately, they were not at the house on that occasion and the housekeeper informed me they were in Paris. An opportunity lost, in my opinion!

By this time, Gogo's two daughters were adults and celebrities themselves. The elder, Marisa Berenson, born in New York on 15 February 1947, became a model and later an actress. The younger Berinthia, or 'Berry', was born in New York on 14 April 1948, and became a renowned photographer and married actor Anthony Perkins on 9 August 1973,

Our return visit to England and Europe, 1951. RIGHT: lunching in Denmark;
in Spakenburg, Holland; in Venice. ABOVE LEFT: Gogo Berenson in San Moritz, Switzerland.

Gogo's daughters 'Berry' Berenson (*left*), Marisa Berenson.

and they had two children together. Both sisters became prominent members of the American social scene. Sadly, Berry died aged fifty-three aboard the American Airlines Flight 11, which crashed into the first of the World Trade Center Towers on 11 September 2001. I remained in regular contact with Gogo until she died in 2011.

Tom and I never returned to India together, but maintained contact with Bhaiya and his sister Ayesha – both of whom kept houses in London where we met up with them regularly, often during Ascot week when we would have an apartment in Sloane Street. The fortunes of Bhaiya and his sister Ayesha changed considerably, like so many others after the grant of Indian independence in 1947. For a time the royal states continued much as before, though merged with neighbouring states, but eventually Bhaiya ceded full power over Cooch Behar to the Indian government on 12 September 1949 and the state became part of West Bengal on 1 January 1950. Bhiaya married the actress Nancy Valentine in 1949, but they separated in 1952. In 1956 he married Georgina May Egan in London, and she became recognised as the Maharani in 1960. Bhaiya died in a light plane crash on 11 April 1970 just before the Indian government stripped the maharajahs of their right to the privy purse in

1971. He had no heirs, so his nephew inherited his title. Coincidentally, his brother-in-law, Jai, Maharajah of Jaipur, died soon afterwards on 24 June 1970, suffering a heart attack on a polo field while umpiring a game in London. The loss of the two men closest to her – and in such a short time – devastated Ayesha. Ayesha, who had grown up with 400 servants, bagged her first leopard at the age of thirteen and survived the abolition of the royal states, entered parliament in 1962 with 'the largest majority of anyone of any parliament of anywhere in the world', retaining her seat at elections in 1967 and 1971. Ayesha visited Australia and stayed with Tom and me and I later stayed with her in Jaipur, in India. We remained in contact until she died on 29 July 2009 aged ninety.

Another of my friendships made in India which lasted over the years was that of Enid de Salis, wife of Lieutenant-Colonel Rudolph de Salis who had been military secretary at Government House in Bihar. Enid, a delightful and amusing person, came from a rich and aristocratic family whose beautiful home, Knowlton, and family seat was near Sandwich, Kent. Enid restored Knowlton's lovely old dower house and made it her home. I always stayed with her there on my visits to England. She and Rudolph were made guardians to the three sons of the Maharajah of Jaipur. When Rudolph and Enid later divorced, Enid remained as guardian to the boys. The eldest boy, known as 'Bubbles', is the present Maharajah of Jaipur.

CHAPTER 11

Town Hall Days

Our time in India prepared us for our life when we became involved with the Adelaide City Council. Tom took civic and public responsibilities seriously, and with his interest in local politics, decided to try to enter the City Council. He succeeded, representing Hindmarsh Ward in the Adelaide City Council from July 1949 to 1951. He returned to council in 1957 representing MacDonnell Ward, until being elected an alderman in 1964 and Lord Mayor in July 1968. He remained Lord Mayor until 1971. Tom

Visit of Her Royal Highness the Queen Mother to Adelaide, 1958, when Lancelot Hargraves and Ursula Hargraves were Lord Mayor and Lady Mayoress. I am standing in the middle of the photograph wearing a large white hat.

had been invited to stand for the position of Lord Mayor on several occasions previously, but as we were either going overseas or had something else interrupting our lives, he had been forced to decline. Tom was always very interested in the on-going development of Adelaide.

We were privileged to dine with the Queen when she visited Adelaide in March 1954. On the morning of the Queen's rest day, having spent the previous day in Whyalla, we received a call from her equerry, John Althorp. John Althorp, later Lord Spencer, was the father of Princess Diana. He had become a close friend of ours when ADC to the Governor, Lord Norrie, who was later Governor-General of New Zealand. He said that if the Queen did not feel too tired, she might want to have some people for supper, so would we hold ourselves in readiness? Can a duck swim!? We duly received the call and spent a memorable evening with the Queen and Prince Philip.

Tom and I, with Tom and Nan Barr-Smith, were the only guests other than the Governor, Sir Robert George and his wife Elizabeth. We had met Princess Margaret when on a visit to a polo match at Cowdray, in England, at the post-match barbeque hosted by the Argentinian team at Park House where they were staying. Since we were to be travelling the next day, Tom warned me not to try the punch as he had seen the hosts lacing it with methylated spirits. I took Tom's advice and was amused to see that when we left after midnight Princess Margaret was still batting on strongly. Next day we read that she was unable to attend divine service because of a heavy load of duties the previous day. The Queen confirmed what we had suspected and said that her sister had felt terrible next day, saying she thought that the grog had been laced. I had to pinch myself in wonder that this was the Queen of England talking and laughing with us in such a relaxed manner.

During the dinner I sat next to Prince Philip and Tom next to the Queen. Despite the Queen's apparent informality, as guests we remained very conscious of protocol. We were seated at the dining table but served ourselves from a magnificent buffet. Everyone was holding back and politely saying, 'After you,' at the buffet, so the Queen was left to return to an empty table. The Governor suggested that Tom serve himself immediately after the Queen and return to the table so she was not sitting alone. Tom did this and later commented that he left feeling hungry because he

Lord Mayor and Lady Mayoress of Adelaide.

was careful to take from the buffet the same portions as the Queen and, because she ate so little, he had to fill up on 'fairy bread'. Another feature of the evening was the viewing of newsreels of her visit to date, with her comments frequently at odds with the fawning commentary.

The following night the Queen attended the state dinner and was every inch the monarch and no longer the relaxed woman we had seen the night before. How lucky and honoured we were to have seen this informal side to the monarch and to have witnessed her great sense of humour.

It seemed that our beautiful golden labrador, Hobo, also took a liking to the Queen, and became famous for gatecrashing her garden party on the banks of the Torrens. There was much in the press about the tight security surrounding the event, journalists noting that the only way to get through the scrutiny would be to swim the river. Hobo, having wandered from home saw the crowds and did just this. I was told that my sister-in-law was standing with a group of people all in their garden party finery, when this great wet dog climbed out of the river and started shaking itself. She cried, 'Good heavens, it's Hobo! Look the other way and perhaps he won't recognise us!'

Tom's election to the position of Lord Mayor meant that I became Lady Mayoress. When he told me he had accepted the position I said, 'Why on earth have you done that?' and added, 'I couldn't bear it.' He replied, 'Well, I think you should,' to which I responded, 'Why should I?' He replied, 'Well, I think you should give back to Adelaide what Adelaide's given you.' I asked, 'What on earth has Adelaide given me that it hasn't given anyone else?' to which he replied, 'Well, it gave you *me*.' 'Well, thank you for nothing,' I said rather grumpily.

I was not looking forward to undertaking the position of Lady Mayoress, but I threw myself into the job and soon found great compensations and the work highly rewarding. It meant a total change in lifestyle and was, in fact, like running an office. I would arrive by 9 am at the Town Hall and go through the engagements for the day with Jean Perrin, who was my very capable secretary during my time at the Town Hall. Major tasks included planning the many receptions, the food, and seating plans if it was a formal lunch or dinner, so my days in the Raj certainly came in handy!

The Lady Mayoress versus Neil Armstrong

As a rather reluctant Lady Mayoress the thought of standing up in public and making speeches positively terrified me! Although nothing prepared me for the competition I was to have when making my first speech. I was invited to open a large charity event for St John Ambulance. The event was a luncheon and fashion parade by Le Louvre, Australia's most prestigious fashion house, which took place in the large old dining room of the South Australian Hotel. It was sold out and everyone I knew in Adelaide was coming, which only added to my terror. For my speech I researched and rehearsed it over and over again to memorise it. When the day of my speech finally arrived it so happened that it was the day the first man landed on the moon, an event that rendered everything else rather unimportant! Everyone kept dashing in and out of the dining room to catch the latest on the television or the radio. Tom was a very good speaker and advised me that I should open with a joke. 'Start with a joke!' I exclaimed, 'I will hardly be able to get out my speech let alone tell jokes!' Yet I refused to let Neil Armstrong beat me completely. Mini skirts had just come into fashion, much to the outrage of many. So I took a deep breath, rose to my feet and said, 'I am sure that you will all be delighted to hear that Miss Wightman has assured me that there are no mini skirts in the parade today . . . I believe a young man recently went to call for his girlfriend and she opened the door to greet him wearing one of the new minis. He said in horror, "What on earth have you got on?" "Oh, just something I threw on in a hurry," she said. "Well, you jolly nearly missed!" he replied.' It wasn't on parr with the moon landing, but it did grab enough attention for me to have an enthusiastic audience remaining. The 20 July 1969 is remembered by all mankind, but it has an even greater significance for me!

As Lord Mayor and Lady Mayoress, we tried to make sure that anyone who had made some contribution to the City of Adelaide had an invitation at some stage during the year. We had a wonderful children's fancy dress party, where children from various homes and orphanages were invited and a wonderful time was had; there were games, a parade of all the costumes and a sumptuous feast.

Over the years I had also become aware that the widows of men who had been prominent in business or some other capacity found that invitations to many events in which they had customarily been invited to with their husbands, declined dramatically. As wives, who by supporting their husbands were also making a significant contribution to society, we felt they should continue to be recognised, and so we inaugurated an annual party for these now elderly women. This usually took the form of a luncheon, but on one memorable occasion when they had all arrived at the Town Hall, during drinks in the Queen Adelaide Room I announced that we were all going down to have lunch on the river on the little boat *Popeye*. Instead of the cries of delight which I had expected, I received a chorus of objections and excuses. 'Oh, June, I couldn't possibly do that because I need my stick,' or 'Oh, but I don't think I could do that. I think it will be too much for me.' I replied, 'Well look, we'll be driven down to the river and back afterwards, the cars will remain there and those who find things too difficult will be driven home.' I had arranged everything and hired *Popeye* for the day. I had George, the Adelaide Club butler, direct a small staff of butlers and waitresses on board and I had also arranged to obtain little trays used on the aircraft from Trans Australian Airlines. The guests reluctantly agreed to go. Once on board *Popeye* everyone was served champagne and lunches were brought around on the trays. We travelled downstream towards the weir and returned to Elder Park, but

Dinner in the Queen Adelaide Room, Adelaide Town Hall.
Back row, facing camera: Tom, centre, me at right.

now nobody wanted to get off. We then went upstream and returned for coffee. All seemed to have forgotten about their sticks and I had to keep running after them saying, 'You left your stick behind on the boat.' They had a wonderful time and I learned that many of them later took picnic lunches and travelled on *Popeye* themselves.

When Tom became Lord Mayor he asked me if I could do something about what he considered was the awful food served at the Town Hall. The staff who dealt with this were initially rather sniffy about my changes. Much of the food I cooked at home I would bring in as a sample. When they discovered it was rather good, I found I had to stop them enthusiastically saying to guests at receptions, 'Oh do have this, the Lady Mayoress cooked this.' Nevertheless, the catering improved and everyone was happy.

As Lady Mayoress I met many people from all walks of life. At functions that I thought would be so boring, I met people who turned out to be most interesting. Most people respected the office of the Lord Mayoralty and felt very diffident to meet the Lord Mayor and Lady Mayoress but we felt very privileged to meet these people.

Tom and I tried to take some of the stuffiness out of the roles of Lord Mayor and Lady Mayoress. Tom signalled the new direction when he arranged to have the 1968 Christmas civic reception at the Adelaide Zoo. He was president of the Zoological Society Council at the time and believed it would be a good idea to reintroduce many of the 500 invitees to the zoo and its work. There was some apprehension, however, with one person who was involved in the planning asking, 'But what about the smell?' Wryly, Tom replied that he had been assured by zoo officials that the animals would not mind. The event turned out to be such a great success that Dr Bruce Eastick, then the Leader of the Opposition in the South Australian Parliament, held his Christmas press party at the zoo four years later.

During Tom's tenure as Lord Mayor, I also supervised arrangements for civic receptions. Guests during this time included Richard Casey – now Lord Casey and Governor-General – who made an official visit to Adelaide. Having left India, Casey returned to federal politics in December 1949 when he was elected to represent La Trobe and appointed Minister for Supply and Development. He was made a life peer in January 1960 and

Tom and I with the Duke and Duchess of Kent, Adelaide Town Hall, 1969.

resigned from the ministry and parliament. He was sworn in as Governor-General on 22 September 1965 and served in the position until April 1969. Casey lived in retirement with his wife Maie at Berwick, outside Melbourne. He died on 17 June 1976 at St Vincent's Hospital, Fitzroy.

The organisation for the Lord Mayor's Ball was colossal, and I asked Stan Ostoja-Kotkowski, a celebrated artist and stage designer, to help me. I told him I wanted his design for the Hall to be a cross between the mirrored halls at Versailles and the ballroom scene in *My Fair Lady*. And Stan did not let me down. Stan also helped me create another wonderful setting for a dinner for 400 guests, which we gave for the Duke and Duchess of Kent in 1969. He featured fictitious heraldic emblems in all the niches and arranged silver on the ceiling that reflected tiny lights

ABOVE AND BELOW: Stan Ostoja-Kotkowski's Town Hall decorations
on the visit of the Duke and Duchess of Kent, 1969.

RIGHT: Tom and I with the Duke of Edinburgh, Adelaide Town Hall, 1970.

BELOW: Tom and I with Sir Ian Bowater, Mayor of London, and his wife Ursula, Adelaide Town Hall, 1970.

hanging below it. I gave one of the guests at each table a list of the seating changes to be made after the main course so people could get to meet one another. The evening did not begin auspiciously. The Duke and Duchess arrived at the Town Hall about three minutes early while we were all inside making last-minute arrangements. When told of their arrival we shot out and saw them milling in the crowded foyer. I was devastated and forgot everyone's names during the introductions! However, the situation was retrieved and everyone seemed to enjoy themselves. The Duke and Duchess stayed longer than scheduled, and the band even had to be asked to stay overtime.

The visit of Sir Ian Bowater, Mayor of London, and his wife Ursula in 1970, remains forever in my memory. We had never met the Bowaters before, so when sitting down to dinner and seeking common ground for conversation, Tom opened by asking Ursula Bowater about her home in England. Her reply led Tom to comment, 'We have great friends, the Weatherbys near Waddon in Buckinghamshire who live nearby.' 'Oh,' she said, 'they're great friends of ours. I'm godmother to Clare Weatherby,' to which Tom replied, 'Well, I'm godfather to Roger Weatherby.' The conversation carried on from there and we became great friends with the Bowaters and visited them whenever we were in England.

In our roles as Lord Mayor and Lady Mayoress we were invited to various gatherings and functions virtually every night, whether at the Town Hall or other centres about town, though Tom made a point of not encroaching on the areas of other mayors. There was one period when we were out thirty-nine nights in succession! There were also various presentations to be made. There was an annual golf day held at the North Adelaide Golf Course, where players contended for the Lord Mayor's Golf Trophy. I suggested to council that there should be a Lady Mayoress's Trophy. The councillors considered this a good idea. I had expected the council would fund the trophy, but it seemed that was not to be the case. So I acquired a most beautiful antique silver rose bowl, which I gave and which is contested annually. The event became such an important match that it became the selection trial for the state team each year.

Much of the work of the council was concerned with routine issues, although there were significant developments during Tom's mayor-alty. He was particularly keen to enhance the amenity of the parklands and encouraged the planting of many trees. He also had the honour of opening the swimming centre in the north parklands and being involved in decisions concerning construction of the Festival Centre. Debate about the Centre had continued for much of the time Tom had been on council. None doubted the need for such a facility, but its location remained an issue until Premier Steele Hall's government settled on a site in Elder Park near the railway station overlooking the River Torrens. Tom had the honour of turning the first sod of soil in March 1970. There now remained the issue of funding. I remember Tom coming home and telling me that he had gone to see Don Dunstan soon after he had become premier in June 1970 to push the idea of the theatre. He emphasised that the council wanted to support it but pointed out that government money was necessary and work could not start in earnest until it was forth-coming. Tom said that Dunstan's reply was: 'Go ahead, what are you waiting for?' Consequently matters began to move quickly after that, and Tom launched a public appeal for funds. We both took great delight when the Festival Theatre was opened by Prime Minister Gough Whitlam on 2 June 1973. Once it had been completed we presented the Centre Trust with a showcase of memorabilia and, when the Festival Theatre foyer was later remodelled, my nephew James and I funded an enlarged showcase.

We completed our terms as Lord Mayor and Lady Mayoress with a sense of relief, and planned to take on no engagements for at least a year.

Tom receiving a gift from William Hayes, his successor as Lord Mayor of Adelaide, 1971.

It had been rare that we had two nights at home to ourselves during the week, and there were times when we had three engagements in one day. And I certainly did not miss the need to give speeches. I had spent countless nights worrying about a speech – I would research, write my own speeches and learn them by heart, then promptly forget the lot once I was on my feet! The end of the term also meant that I did not have to buy so many clothes, not that I have ever found that a hardship as I was no longer in the public eye. However, Tom and I both felt it had been a great honour to have had the opportunity to serve the City of Adelaide.

After the Town Hall

Tom was able to contribute little to day-to-day management of his business while serving as Lord Mayor, although by this time his staff had grown considerably and there were senior partners who had no need for his constant attention. Still, he regularly spent time in the office in the

Tom and I attending a reception for the Queen and Prince Philip.

evenings after discharging his civic responsibilities, especially during the share market rally fuelled by speculative mining stocks in the period after 1966. The speculative mania that gripped Adelaide, particularly after the interest generated by nickel producer Poseidon, certainly created a great deal of work in the office.

I continued to be involved in charity work after my stint as Lady Mayoress, and one memorable occasion was when I chaired a committee formed to organise a fundraising ball for the Crippled Children's Association on 8 September 1972. Governor Sir Mark Oliphant, patron of the Association, was good enough to allow us to use Government House, where we erected a large marquee and decorated it to reflect a medieval theme. The event was devised and overseen by Sydney designer Ray Siede of Double Bay, and featured heraldic devices, suits of armour and canopies. There were massed flares to light the drive with the 600 guests being waited on by costumed pages and serving wenches and servants in scarlet tunics. The press described the event variously as, 'A night to remember at Government House', and 'The ball of the century'.

Tom was a member of the Liberal Party but was never tempted nor had the desire to enter state or federal politics – I certainly would have been against it! Still, he had close dealings and warm relations with a succession of premiers from Tom Playford to Don Dunstan. David Tonkin, Premier from September 1979 to November 1982, asked if he could put Tom's name forward for the position of Governor of South Australia. Tom was honoured, but not especially keen on the idea. He discussed it with me and I echoed his reluctance. We had not had much time to ourselves while he was Lord Mayor, and we anticipated even less time together if he became Governor. There were times, however, when we assisted Government House.

On one occasion we suddenly found ourselves unexpectedly having to play host to a Government House guest. Lady Brabourne, who was the Dowager Countess of Brabourne, was coming to Australia and doing a 'grand tour' of all the Government Houses, including Adelaide. Various mutual friends of ours in England had written saying they had given her our name, and would we meet up with her and perhaps entertain her. Before Lady Brabourne arrived I had a call from Lady Bastian, the wife of the Governor at the time, asking if Lady Brabourne could stay with us since the Queen Mother had recently been staying at Government House and all the staff had been given holidays after. Lady Bastian would listen to none of my excuses as to why Lady Brabourne could not stay with us, and matters were further complicated when I suddenly lost my house staff and could find no extra help. I wondered how on earth I would cope. When Lady Brabourne arrived in the Government House car, I ushered her upstairs to the guest room, where I always kept an iron and ironing board in the cupboard for guests' use, and I said, 'Lady Brabourne, if you want any ironing done . . .' But she did not give me a chance to finish before saying, 'Just a moment and I will give it to you.' She opened her suitcase and took out a mass of washing and ironing and handed it to me. We went out to dinner that evening and, after we had returned and the others had gone upstairs to bed, I vanished downstairs. Tom followed me down and said, 'What are you doing?' I replied, 'Well, I'm being upstairs Nellie. I only hope I get the tip.' I finished the washing and ironing before going to bed exhausted.

The next morning I took Lady Brabourne her breakfast tray and sat on the end of the bed and chatted to her for a while. At about 11 am she came downstairs and I served coffee in the garden under the oak tree. After putting down the tray and chatting for a moment or two, I exclaimed, 'Oh, I think I can hear the phone, excuse me,' whereupon I rushed upstairs to make the bed, tidy the room, clean the bath and mop the floor. This happened every morning. This rigmarole went on for the week and by this time we had become close friends so I could not tell her the truth as I knew it would embarrass her. Before she left we had a dinner party in her honour, and although I had George the butler from the Adelaide Club and Doris and Alice to help serve, I had risen early to prepare all the food myself. Just before leaving she said, 'June, I have two things I must say to you. The first thing is that I could not have loved staying with you and Tom more than I have done, it has been marvellous. And secondly, you know I have stayed in all the great houses of the world, and I have never stayed anywhere where they have better servants. They are all so quiet and everything is so beautifully done. But I haven't seen anyone. What do I do about the tip?' I replied, 'Oh, simply leave it on the dressing table,' and I remarked to Tom, 'and I'm not too proud to take it!'

All my friends in England knew the story, but I implored them not to tell Lady Brabourne and embarrass her. The next time we went to England she had an enormous party for us and told all the dukes, duchesses and ambassadors who were present that whenever they travelled to Australia they should stay with us because we had such good staff. Unfortunately, she came to an untimely end. Her son had married Pamela *Patricia* Mountbatten, the daughter of Lord and Lady Mountbatten. Lady Brabourne had been with Lord Louis Mountbatten when terrorists at Mullaghmore, in Northern Ireland, blew up his yacht on 27 August 1979. She died of injuries the following day. *fishing boat*

Tom was recognised for his many public roles when he was appointed a Knight Bachelor in the Queen's Birthday Honours list on 3 June 1978 for services to local government. I was surprised when I learned about his appointment and queried him on why he accepted this honour when he had previously avoided any public recognition. I was very moved by his response that he considered anything he had done in life had only been with my assistance, and so accepted it, 'Because it was the only honour I have ever been offered which included you.'

We travelled to Buckingham Palace for the investiture. It was a disappointment that Tom's godson Roger Weatherby was unable to come along as our guest because he could not get permission to leave Eton for the occasion. So our dear friend, his mother Alison, accompanied us instead. The ceremony was a simple one – all the guests were seated in the hall and those to be honoured approached the Queen, one by one, from a side room, and were touched on the shoulder with the sword. After a word or two from the Queen, they moved aside for the next recipient. We hosted a lunch party after at the famous London club Boodles and our many English friends joined us to celebrate.

This was about the time Tom considered retiring. The Australia-wide recession in the early 1980s brought continued changes to the Adelaide Stock Exchange and prompted a rationalisation of Adelaide's broking businesses, which included F.W. Porter & Co. Also, Tom's health began to deteriorate, and after forty years managing the business, he believed it was time for a change. Consequently, F.W. Porter & Co. merged with S.V.B. Day & Co. in July 1982 to form S.V.B. Day Porter & Co.

At Buckingham Palace after Tom's knighthood had been conferred, 1978.

Continuing interests

Ballet continued to be a passion of mine. I had always been interested in ballet right from the time of my debut with Twinkle Blau at Kambala, and while I did not have ballet classes at Kobeelya, I always retained a great interest and attended the ballet whenever possible. Not long after I finished school my parents took me to see the Russian Ballet in Perth. I also took ballet lessons after Tom and I returned to Adelaide. I went to Joanne Priest, who had what she called her 'mum's class', for mature students who wished to take their exercise in an activity they loved. I attended once a week for several years.

When the Australian Ballet became an autonomous body – after having been under the auspices of the Elizabethan Theatre Trust – chairman Dick Seddon rang me from Melbourne. Tom and I had already received a letter inviting us to be members of the newly formed Australian Ballet Foundation, and Dick Seddon said he hoped we would accept the invitation to join. Then he said to me, 'We want to know if you would go a step further and come on the board?' I was so surprised and replied, 'Oh, good heavens, I don't think I could do that. I don't think I've anything to offer.' He responded, 'Well, we think you have and we would like you to do so.' I said, 'Well, I'll think about it.' I did not know why they thought I would be a good candidate, but they knew I loved the ballet. I suggested various other people instead, but they were adamant. So I accepted and remained on the board for eighteen years. Fellow board members were Chairman Dick Sedden, Sir Ian Potter, Professor Fred Alexander from Perth and Isla Burnside from Melbourne, who made a great contribution and was a member from the very beginning.

Ballet for me has all of the arts wrapped up in one – every time the curtain goes up the scene resembles a beautiful painting, there is the poetry of motion of beautiful bodies, and there is, of course, the exquisite music. I have had the privilege of seeing and, I hope, of having some part in this young national company develop to become one of the most acclaimed companies in the world. I have been able to learn and appreciate the enormous energy, work and dedication that is given not only by all the dancers, but scene shifters bumping in and out of theatres, loading the trucks to get all on for the next venue, both interstate and overseas; the wardrobe department making the beautiful costumes and head-dresses and cleaning, washing, repairing and generally caring for them between performances; physiotherapists; masseurs and the other people who care for the well-being of the dancers' bodies. I saw, too, the wonderful education program that the Company took out into the schools and the Ballet School, which has become such an integral part of the Company.

The founding of the Company depended upon the energy and enthusiasm of Dame Peggy Van Praagh, the founding director. This was followed in 1962 with Dame Margaret Scott founding and becoming the Director of the Australian Ballet School. As a result of their achievements, Australian dancers are now sought after in all the world's top companies.

I was always closely involved with the members of the Company, and was instrumental in the development of the Ballet Centre. I travelled to Melbourne the day before board meetings and spent time with the Company. Originally working from a condemned building at the former Presbyterian Ladies' College in East Melbourne, the company moved to a converted tyre factory at Flemington in 1968. This proved far from ideal. Water would pour in through the roof whenever it rained and we would have buckets everywhere. Unfortunately, because of competing demands for funds, the idea of a purpose-built ballet centre was always low on the board's action plans. However, Isla Burnside and I decided it was important to make a stand, and proclaimed that we would not leave the meeting until a definite decision was made as to whether or not to build an appropriate centre. After much discussion, there was a unanimous decision to go ahead and build the Australian Ballet Centre. The excitement when the news came out was so intense with everyone, including Mary the tea lady, running around and exclaiming: 'We're going to have our really own ballet centre!' Our attention then turned to the big job of acquiring land (which was finally found next to the Arts Centre in Melbourne), designing a centre that would include the school and costume department, soliciting government grants and the enormous job of raising funds. To everyone's great joy, Prime Minister Bob Hawke opened the Australian Ballet Centre at a gala event on 18 February 1988.

During my time on the board of the Australian Ballet it came under the directorships of Dame Peggy Van Praagh, who then for some time was co-director with Sir Robert Helpmann (this in many minds, certainly mine, created a two-headed monster and I was of the opinion that Peggy did all the work and Bobbie turned up in time for the curtain call); Maina Guilgard; Ann Woolliams from Stuttgart, whose association with John Cranko was able to bring to us his lovely *Romeo and Juliet* and *Onegin*; Marilyn Jones, previously our talented principal dancer; and then the joint partnership of Marilyn Rowe and Marilyn Jones. During this time I was to see the highs and lows of the Company.

The lowest time was when the Company went on strike for twenty-six days in October 1981, forcing the cancellation of the Brisbane season and parts of the seasons in Melbourne and Sydney. When Marilyn Jones was appointed artistic director, one of our very talented dancers, Kelvin Coe, became disgruntled at not receiving the appointment himself. He, along with some of the principal dancers set out to undermine Marilyn's authority, and she began to lose the level of discipline necessary for a ballet company. Rather than directly target Marilyn for their discontent, they chose general manager Peter Bahen, who managed the finances and contributed greatly to creating the finances required for the Company's ongoing needs. But Peter had a matter-of-fact and abrasive manner that could upset finely attuned artistic people. Matters were further exacerbated by the aggressive attitude of the union representative to the Company, and so we were finding it very difficult to come to a reasonable understanding.

The Company was demanding that Marilyn go as well as Peter, paving the way for Kelvin to take over the artistic directorship. This resulted in many meetings, often late, and much waiting around in the draughty corridors of the arbitration court. I would often go to Melbourne for a meeting, taking with me a little overnight bag, saying to Tom, 'I don't know when you can expect to see me again.' As I have always had a good personal relationship with all members of the Company, many of whom had not been happy with the way things were going throughout the strike but admired and respected the principals, would ring me and keep me informed of the thinking of the strike's leaders. The board realised that Marilyn needed support, and we contacted several artists who were overseas, but who were unable to come because of their existing commitments at the time.

Things were becoming very tense with no solution in sight. Then one Saturday morning, I had a frenzied telephone call from one of my friends in the Company telling me that the strike committee had determined to disband the Company at next Monday's meeting at the arbitration court. They had received offers from the great entrepreneur, Michael Edgley, and seemed to believe that they could reform under a different banner. I was distraught at the thought of losing all that Peggy Van Praagh had done to form this brilliant national company, and decided that there was only one person who could work with Marilyn Jones and save the Company. That person was Marilyn Rowe, our former beautiful principal dancer who had gone into retirement and seclusion after her husband, Christopher Maver, had been tragically killed in a plane crash when returning from Sydney after one of the Company's performances. I rang Bob Southey, the chairman, but he had gone trout fishing in the Snowy Mountains. Then I tried calling Fred Millar, the vice-chairman, who was out riding on his property. In desperation I rang Joy Sneddon, a fellow board member and said, 'Joy I really think we will have to take the matter into our own hands and contact Marilyn and ask her if she would be agreeable to come back.' We spent the whole weekend on the telephone and by Sunday afternoon Marilyn had agreed.

The next morning I arrived early to the meeting and told the board what I had done and they were delighted. We set off to the arbitration court and confronted the grim and determined little group, consisting of a lot of nervous young dancers all wondering if they would have a company at the conclusion of the meeting. We discussed the situation with them and asked that if we could give them someone who would come and work *with* Marilyn as co-director to get the company running again according to the standards and conditions expected, would they agree to go back to work. We could see from the way the spokesmen for the dancers replied, that they did not believe we had a person to which they would agree. When we said 'Marilyn Rowe' there was a deathly silence and they asked us to leave the room while they took a vote. As we left the room to wait once more in the cold and draughty passageway, I saw Kelvin Coe turn to the person next to him and say, 'We've lost.' The voting quickly over, we returned to a 'Yes' vote.

Now we were faced with the problem of the final performance at the

Sydney Opera House before Christmas. It was decided that the performance would be the *Merry Widow* since it did not need as much rehearsal time. This was a performance I will never forget. We had our lovely Marilyn back working with the Company, the Company was saved and dancing on stage and the performance of the romantic *Merry Widow* was an enormous success. After the performance we were all crying and hugging each other back stage and I remember one of the principal dancers saying to me as we clung to each other in tears, 'You'll get covered in grease paint,' and me tearfully replying, 'I don't care.'

With the dark days of the strike behind us, the Australian Ballet went from strength to strength. Marilyn Rowe later successfully took on the role as director of the Australian Ballet School, thereby ensuring the healthy future of the Australian Ballet Company.

At the premiere of the Australian Ballet's gala performance of *Merry Widow* at the Kennedy Center, New York, with, (*left to right*), Hubert Humphrey and Nelson Rockefeller. (Photograph by Richard Braaten)

I travelled with the ballet on several occasions. I went to Russia where the Company performed *Romeo and Juliet*. The first night we danced at the Marinski Theatre in Leningrad, a most beautiful theatre with a tiny stage. I did not realise that Russians did not normally clap individual performances, and so on the first night the company danced beautifully to be met with a deathly silence after solos and duets. I remember thinking, 'They don't like us, this is terrible.' But, when they came forward to take the curtain call at the end, the audience rose as one and absolutely erupted. Company members at first thought they were going to be lynched, until they realised the audience was applauding. After that, the Australian Ballet could do no wrong in Russia, and ever since there has almost always been a member of the Australian Ballet as guest principal with the Bolshoi or another Russian ballet company.

I also travelled with the company to England when it performed *Sleeping Beauty* at Covent Garden for the Royal Command Performance, as well as through Malaysia and Taiwan. Tom and I had previously been to America for the company's gala performance of *Merry Widow* at the Kennedy Center in Washington with Margot Fonteyn as guest artist. Margot Fonteyn was guest artist for the Australian Ballet on many occasions and was as charming and gracious as she was a great artist. I was both honoured and delighted when I was elected an Honorary Life Member of the Australian Ballet on 5 April 2000.

Other activities

Having travelled so much overseas, and mindful of my lack of knowledge of history and art during our first visit to Europe, I determined to go to university to study fine arts. I had hoped to gain one of three places open to mature-age students at Flinders University, but was not successful. So it was suggested that I gain entry by means of a mature-age pathway and do so under the provisional matriculation scheme. I enrolled as a Bachelor of Arts student to study fine arts, English literature and French. I loved university life and I believe I fitted in well with the younger students. I lunched with them when I was on campus and had interesting political discussions with them. I may have seemed like a stuffy old conservative, but I relished the debate. Those with whom I studied were delighted when I passed, and were keen for me to continue in their seminar group the following year. At the end of my first year I received a letter from the university indicating that my grades in first year were sufficiently high to give me matriculation status. I was proud of my achievement, having not completed my secondary schooling. I did not have the chance to complete the degree, however, as Tom became extremely ill with heart trouble during my second year, and was given little chance of recovering. I opted to spend our remaining time together nursing him.

CHAPTER 12

After Tom

It transpired that Tom never recovered his health, and died at Cosford on 23 July 1983, just eighteen days after his seventieth birthday, never having lost his sense of fun or his consideration for those around him. I sat by his bed and was as cold as the hand I held and my heart turned to stone. But the wonderful journey we had been on together would remain vividly engraved in my heart and memory forever. He was farewelled by friends at a service in Christ Church, North Adelaide, before another service at Centennial Park.

I now had many decisions to make about the remainder of my life. I decided that a complete change of lifestyle that would allow little time for grieving was required. I wanted to continue my French studies so went to live in Paris for a time. Gogo lived in Paris and wanted me stay with her, but I told her that we would speak only English together. So Gogo organised for me to stay with Chantal de Crissy, an artist friend of hers who lived in Neuilly. I enrolled in Eurocentre, on Rue Dauphine on the Left Bank, and went in early each morning on the metro to attend lectures all day. After, I would dine with Gogo or other friends in Paris. Happily I was able to continue to pursue my love of ballet, and to my great delight to see the Roland Petit Ballet Company. After spending a couple of months in Paris I travelled on to England and stayed with friends there.

After my time away, I felt I was now able to return to Adelaide to face life on my own with renewed vigour and purpose. My nieces and nephews feared that I might return to Perth, but Adelaide had been my home for over forty years. While I still had close friends in Perth, they were also getting older and I was satisfied that I could visit them when I wished. Also, my sister Shirley remained in Adelaide.

My most immediate task was to work out what to do with Cosford. It was impractical to continue living in such a big house by myself and no one in the family was keen to acquire it. Sadly, I decided there was no alternative but to sell. But before doing so, I arranged to subdivide the land into large blocks with covenants on each to ensure they could not be subdivided further and spoil the appreciation of the house. I also kept one quarter-acre block, which had been the rose garden, in the hope that someone in the family might one day wish to build there.

Faced with living by myself I did not want to live in a large house surrounded by garden, and decided that an apartment was the answer to my needs. To find an apartment I liked became a challenge as I had very definite ideas on what I wanted. Eventually I made the decision to build and get exactly what I wanted. I had an agent do a door knock in my preferred neighbourhoods, and in the process met Henry O'Connor, who had recently acquired a house in Bagot Street, North Adelaide, with the intention of demolishing it and building a block of flats. I approached him and asked if he would build what I wanted. The individual apartments I wanted were much larger than he had planned and he doubted that others would be interested in buying them. I offered to fund the apartments if built to my specifications, on his land. He agreed, and we had a very amicable joint venture. I drew up the plans I wanted and his architect built the four apartments exactly as I designed, and we had no trouble selling the other three.

I remained at Cosford for two-and-a half years while the apartment block was being built, finally moving there in 1986. I was reluctant to sell the tiger and leopard rugs that had graced the billiard room and reminded me of my days in India, but there was insufficient room for them in my new home and no one in the family wanted them. Cosford eventually passed to Robert Champion de Crespigny, but only after he had persuaded me to sell him my remaining block of land.

Before leaving Cosford, I had a Sunday lunch and invited all known descendants of J.W. Porter, who had built Cosford. We had 280 cousins, the oldest being Ethel Verco aged eighty-two, and the youngest her great-granddaughter, Sarah, aged only a few months. Also, on the following Friday, I had guests arrive from Melbourne, Sydney, Perth and England for the dinner-dance I gave for 400 friends in the garden on the Saturday night. On the Sunday I engaged a bus and my friends with cars to transport my visitors and me to Hugh and Fiona McLachlan's property Glendevon, near Williamstown, where they had kindly offered to have

On the terrace at the new 'Cosford', North Adelaide.

us all. I arranged for caterers to provide a picnic lunch, which we enjoyed around their swimming pool. This weekend became known as my 'three-day event'.

I named my new apartment block Cosford for sentimental reasons. Since I was no longer entertaining on the scale I did while Tom was alive, the apartment proved suitable for the smaller dinner parties I continued to host. I also remained involved in various charities, although increasingly as a supporter as opposed to an active fundraiser. For instance, I became a member of the Collectors' Club of the Art Gallery of South Australia, where each of us contributed to a common fund. We have an annual dinner where each curator presents the members with a list of works that he or she wishes to acquire for their particular section of the

ABOVE: Nephew James Porter escorting me to my 90th birthday celebrations, Adelaide, 2009.

LEFT: With my great-niece Edwina at my 90th birthday celebrations, Adelaide, 2009. Edwina is wearing one of my old ball gowns.

gallery and which they believed would enhance the gallery. The members then viewed each of the works put forward and voted for the ones they believe should be acquired. The items attracting the greatest number of votes are purchased. The Art Gallery of South Australia is a gem, and I enjoy my many visits and appreciate the work and time its curators put into it.

After Tom I also continued to travel a great deal and was lucky to have friends who invited me to join them on their travels. I visited most countries in Europe and South America, as well as Cambodia, Bhutan, Nepal and Delhi, which I had not visited during my time in India. I also went hot-air ballooning in France and returned later to stay with Gogo and Gino in Santa Margherita.

The palaces in which I have stayed, the maharajahs whose guest I have been, the fabulous jewels, the elephant rides through the jungle, now seem like a fairytale, especially as they are now mostly lost to the realms of history – a history of which I was fortunate to be a part. My memories of the Raj remain vivid, as do the friendships and experiences that enriched my life. And I never cease to be amazed at the role Fate played. If asked would I live my life all over again, my answer would most definitely be 'Can a duck swim?!'

Afterword

As I mention at the beginning, I have used my own diaries and letters and those of my husband Tom to assist in chronicling these memoirs. I intend to deposit these in the State Library of South Australia where others might read them should they be interested.

I have also used information from many other sources.

Particular books from which I have garnered details include various volumes of the *Australian Dictionary of Biography* for biographical information; R.G. Casey, *An Australian in India*, Hollis & Carter, London 1947; G. Bywater, 'War Task: R.G. Casey's Governorship of Bengal, 1944–1945', BA (Hons) Thesis, Flinders University of South Australia, 1981; and Rob Linn, *Those Turbulent Years: a history of the City of Adelaide, 1929–1979*, Adelaide City Council, Adelaide, 2006.

My friend Gayatri Devi of Jaipur with Santha Rama Rau, wrote *A Princess Remembers*, Century Publishing, London, 1976, from which I have drawn. The life and adventures of Boris Lissanevitch is told by Michel Peissel in *Tiger for Breakfast: The Story of Boris of Xathmandu*, E.P. Dutton & Co, New York, 1966, and available on the internet; details of Sydney de Kantzow have been gleaned from the website devoted to the history of the China National Aviation Corporation that is moderated by Tom O. Moore Jr; background on the Raj Darbhanga jewels can be found in the blog by Akshay Chavan, titled 'Indian Royalty, Maharajahs and more . . .'

Acknowledgements

To my dear friend, the late Rajmata of Jaipur, who died in 2010, and who was the first to sow the seed in my mind of writing about my experiences of living during the last days of the British Raj.

To my dear friend Frances, the Countess zu Stolberg, who's faith in my ability and constant 'nagging' encouraged me to get going.

To the Jiminy Cricket perpetually on my shoulder to make sure that the 'little duck kept swimming', Marina Hamilton Craig.

To my nephew, James Porter, who finally pushed me over the edge and introduced me to the Donovans.

Peter 'Sleuth' Donovan now knows more about me than I know about me, and not only verified all historical facts, but was able to extend the knowledge in my letters and diaries.

To June Donovan, who showed the most unbelievable patience in typing while I tried to decipher and read my indecipherable writing, without her help I doubt if I would have made it.

To the staff at the State Library of South Australia for their assistance.

Akshay Chavan, from India, has corrected some infelicities, and facilitated access to photographs of Maharajah Kameshwar Singh from the Kalyani Foundation in Darbhanga, Bihar, India.

To Tejkar Jha for access to photographs from the Kalyani Foundation in Darbhanga, Bihar, India.

To Peter de Kantzow for photographs of his father and mother.

To the Australian Ballet for providing photographs.

To Michael Ross, who has drawn the maps.

To the many friends whose encouragement has kept me going.

The assistance of all and permission to publish photographs is acknowledged and greatly appreciated.

Wakefield Press is an independent publishing and
distribution company based in Adelaide, South Australia.
We love good stories and publish beautiful books.
To see our full range of books, please visit our website at
www.wakefieldpress.com.au
where all titles are available for purchase.